POCKET

MONEY

The Economist Desk Companion
The Economist Economics
The Economist Guide to Economic Indicators
The Economist Guide to the European Union
The Economist Numbers Guide
The Economist Style Guide
The Guide to Analysing Companies
The Guide to Financial Markets
The Guide to Management Ideas
The Dictionary of Economics
The International Dictionary of Finance
Going Digital
Improving Marketing Effectiveness
Management Development
Managing Complexity
Measuring Business Performance

Pocket Accounting
Pocket Advertising
Pocket Director
Pocket Finance
Pocket Economist
Pocket International Business Terms
Pocket Internet
Pocket Investor
Pocket Law
Pocket Manager
Pocket Marketing
Pocket MBA
Pocket Negotiator
Pocket Strategy

The Economist Pocket Asia
The Economist Pocket Europe in Figures
The Economist Pocket World in Figures

The
Economist
Books

POCKET
MONEY

THE ECONOMIST IN ASSOCIATION WITH
PROFILE BOOKS LTD

Profile Books Ltd
58A Hatton Garden, London EC1N 8LX
www.profilebooks.co.uk

Published in 2000 by Profile Books Ltd
in association with
The Economist Newspaper Ltd
www.economist.com

Contributors Peter Holden, Ulric Spencer, Jonathan Williams
Material extracted from the *Guide to Economic Indicators*
text copryight © Richard Stutely
Material extracted from the *Guide to Financial Markets*
text copyright © Marc Levinson

Typest in Garamond by MacGuru
info@macguru.org.uk

Printed in Italy by
LEGO S.p.a. – Vicenza – Italy

A CIP catalogue record for this book is available
from the British Library

ISBN 1 86197 156 7

Contents

Introduction

Pocket Money is one of a series of books in a handy format that combine a wealth of factual data with the clarity of explanation and analysis for which *The Economist* is famous. Some of it has been adapted from other *Economist* books, such as the *Guide to Financial Markets* by Marc Levinson and the *Guide to Economic Indicators* but the bulk of the book has been freshly researched and written.

Organised in seven main sections, the book aims to look at all the many aspects of money:

- how it has evolved and how it is evolving
- who uses which currencies
- how much money there is and how its supply is measured and controlled
- the system of exchange rates for valuing one currency against another
- the effect of inflation on the value of money
- the price of gold and silver over time
- the various financial markets – money, foreign exchange, bond, stock and the fast-growing market for derivatives
- the cashless world in which money moves about electronically
- the money governments raise and spend, borrow or give to other countries as aid
- what people earn, what they save and what they spend their money on
- and a final "Miscellamoney" section includes some bits and pieces that we were unable to fit into the earlier sections.

Intended to entertain and amuse as well as to inform, we hope you find *Pocket Money* a fascinating guide to what, according to a famous song "makes the world go round".

PART 1

A BRIEF HISTORY OF MONEY

A chronology of money

West and South Asia

BC
Late 3rd millennium
Earliest records of the use of silver bullion by weight and grain by volume as mediums of exchange and units of value in Mesopotamia

1792–1750
The laws of Hammurabi, king of Babylon, establish ideal prices for various commodities and services in terms of silver and grain

650–600
Coins invented in Lydia (western Turkey) made of electrum (a natural alloy of gold and silver)

About 550
Earliest gold and silver coins made in Lydia

5th century
Gold and silver coins issued in west of Persian Empire

Early 4th century
First silver 'coins' in northern India (stamped silver ingots)

336–323
Alexander the Great conquers the Persian Empire, capturing 180,000 talents (1 talent = 25.8kg) of booty from the royal treasuries, most of which is turned into coin

323–31
Hellenistic period. Greek kingdoms from Egypt to India spread use of coinage in the Near East

3rd century
First cast copper coins in northern India

About 250–early 1st century
Greek kingdom in Afghanistan and northern India issues Greek-style coins, gradually adapted to Indian styles

AD
1st century
Coin production spreads to southern India

and Sri Lanka

1st–4th centuries

Kushan kingdom in north-western India and Pakistan issues Greek-style coinage in gold and bronze

4th–6th centuries

Gupta kingdom in northern India issues coins derived from the Kushans

About 640

First Islamic coinage

696

Early Islamic coinage purged of Byzantine and Iranian influences by Caliph Abd al-Malik. Gold *dinars*, silver *dirhams* and copper *fals* coins are integrated into a system which becomes standard for later Islamic states

1173–1206

Northern India briefly brought under Islamic rule by Ghurid dynasty. Islamic coins issued, integrated with Indian coin systems

1291–95

Mongol Ilkhanid ruler Geikhatu attempts to enforce exclusive use of paper money in Iran. The innovation is a failure

1526–1761

Mughal Empire dominates India, spreading Islamic coinage and the rupee denomination (from Sanskrit *rupyah*, meaning silver)

1671

British East India Company begins issuing rupees in India

1780

Machine-made copper coinage introduced by the British in Calcutta. Advertisements for the coins fixed a rate of 5,120 cowrie shells to 1 silver rupee

1835

Rupee made standard throughout British India. The denomination spreads to South-East Asia, replacing the use of such varied forms of money as human heads and silver and tin ingots, and to British and German colonies in east Africa

1850s–70s
Paper money first introduced in Ottoman and Persian Empires

Africa

BC
Late 3rd millennium
First records of the use of gold, silver and copper bullion by weight as a means of exchange for goods and services and expressing values in Egypt

6th–5th centuries
Greek cities in North Africa begin to make coins

Late 5th–early 4th centuries
Copies of Athenian silver coins made in Egypt in large numbers

Late 4th century
Carthage (modern Tunisia) begins to make coins. Rare gold and silver coins with demotic and hieroglyphic inscriptions made in Egypt

Late 4th–1st centuries
The Ptolemaic Kingdom in Egypt makes an extensive coinage in gold, silver and bronze

1st century BC–1st century AD
North African kingdoms of Mauretania and Numidia produce silver and bronze coins

AD
1st century BC–7th century AD
Roman coins made in huge numbers at Alexandria for circulation in Egypt

Late 3rd–early 6th centuries
The Christian Axumite Kingdom in Ethiopia makes coins

Late 7th century onwards
Islamic gold and bronze coins made in north Africa and Egypt

Early 9th century
Islamic states in Morocco and Tunisia begin striking coins

10th–11th centuries
Gold coinage in northern Islamic states
becomes more common. Sources of gold lie in
Trans-saharan Africa

909–1171
Fatimid dynasty rules in Egypt. Its gold dinars
are of remarkable purity, becoming a standard
Mediterranean trade coin

1171–1250
Ayyubid dynasty rules in Egypt. Recommences
coinage in silver

14th century
An Arab traveller, Ibn Battuta, reports use of
salt as money among inhabitants of kingdom
of Mali

1425
First issue of the *ashrafi*, a pure gold trade
coin intended to compete with the Venetian
ducat. It became a standard term for Islamic
gold coins

15th century
Portuguese traders use copper bracelets
(*manillas*) to purchase slaves in Nigeria. They
continue in use as money until 1940s

18th century
European travellers report the use of rock salt
in Ethiopia

19th century
Cross-shaped copper ingots, camwood and
raffia cloths used as money in central Africa;
cowrie shells used in west Africa

Late 19th–20th centuries
Coin- and banknote-based monetary systems
come to dominate in colonial and post-
colonial Africa

China and East Asia

BC
13th century
Inscriptions in China record the use of cowrie
shells as gifts

650–600

Cast bronze coinage invented in China

475–221

Period of the Warring States. Cast coins made in shapes of knives, hoes and cowrie shells

221

Qin State introduces round cast bronze coin with square hole, which remains standard form for Chinese coins until the late 19th century (known in English as *cash*)

118

Han Dynasty introduces *wuzhu* (five grain) coinage, which becomes standard for the next 700 years

AD

621

Tang Dynasty introduces *kaiyuan tongbao* (meaning 'new beginning, circulating treasure') coinage

708

First coinage in Japan, in Chinese style

960–1279

During Song Dynasty paper exchange notes with date limitation begin to circulate

996

First coinage in Korea, in Chinese style

1206–1367

During Yuan Dynasty paper money circulates exclusively. Marco Polo remarks on it: "When these papers have been so long in circulation that they are growing torn and frayed, they are brought to the mint and changed for new and fresh ones at a discount of 3%. If a man wants to buy gold or silver ... he goes to the Khan's mint with some of these papers and gives them in payment ... All the Khan's armies are paid with this sort of money."

1401

Paper money first issued in Korea

1840s–1930s

Silver ingots (*sycee*) widely used as money in China

1869

First automated mint established in Osaka, Japan, issuing silver dollars

1889

Automated coinage machinery introduced in Canton, issuing silver dollars

1897

Imperial Bank of China founded

1899

First paper dollar notes issued in China

1912

Last issue of traditional bronze Chinese *cash* coins

1912

First issue of Chinese coins with portrait – of President Sun Yat-Sen

1953

Renminbi yuan currency introduced in People's Republic of China

Europe

BC

About 550

Silver coins begin to be made by Greek city states (Aegina, Corinth and Athens the earliest)

About 500

Silver coinage spreads to Greek cities in mainland Greece, Macedonia, the Greek islands, Asia Minor, southern Italy, Sicily, Cyprus and southern France

About 483

Athenians discover rich silver mines at Laurion. They make the famous silver "owl" coinage and build a fleet with which they defeat the Persians at Salamis in 480

About 425

Token bronze coinage introduced in Sicily

Late 4th century

Token bronze coinage introduced in Athens

357

Philip II of Macedon captures the mines at Amphipolis, allowing the production of massive issues of coinage

About 310

Coinage adopted in Rome, in a non-integrated system of cast bronze ingots, cast bronze discs, struck bronze coins and struck silver coins

About 270

First coinage in Celtic Continental Europe (gold and silver coins in France, Germany, Danube region and Balkans)

About 212

Denarius coinage introduced in Rome, a silver denomination which remained standard until circa 240AD

About 80

First coins made in Britain (gold staters in south-east England)

AD

27BC–14AD

Augustus reforms the Roman coinage, establishing a stable quadrimetallic system (gold, silver, brass, copper) which dominates the Roman world for the next 250 years

43

Roman invasion brings to an end indigenous coin production in southern Britain

Middle-late 3rd century

Political and military crisis within the Roman Empire causes inflation, undermining the Roman currency, reducing it to a base-silver coinage of fluctuating value

270–305

Roman emperors Aurelian (270–75) and Diocletian (284–305) establish an empire-wide network of mints for coin production, from London to Antioch

301

Roman emperor Diocletian issues a Price Edict establishing maximum prices for various commodities to put a brake on inflation. It is a failure

About 309

Roman emperor Constantine the Great

introduces the gold *solidus*, which remains standard into the Byzantine period as the "bezant" until the 11th century

4th–5th centuries
Roman currency periodically reformed but inflation persists

476
End of Roman Empire in western Europe. Coinage continues to be produced in gold, silver and bronze by German successor states in Italy, southern France and north Africa, and in gold alone elsewhere. Coinage dies out completely in post-Roman Britain

491–518
Eastern Roman emperor Anastasius reforms the currency; he dies with 320,000 Roman pounds of gold in the treasury

About 600
Anglo-Saxons begin making gold coins in England

About 675
Silver coinage takes over from gold in northern Europe and Britain

About 755
Pepin, king of the Franks, introduces a silver coin, called the *denarius*, which forms the basis for all later European medieval silver penny coinages

9th century
Vikings raid throughout Europe. Their trade and war bring Arab silver coins through Russia into Scandinavia and Britain

About 1000
Silver coinage first made in Scandinavia, Ireland, eastern Europe, Russia

About 1160
Discovery of new silver mines at Freiberg, Saxony, greatly expands the amount of silver in circulation, allowing production of larger coins (often as shillings or their equivalents)

13th century
Rise of north Italian banking houses, known in northern Europe as Lombards (hence Lombard Street)

1251–52

Genoa and Florence launch new gold coinages (the genesis of the florin coinage). Gold coinage spreads across Europe

1284

Venice introduces the *ducat*, a high-value gold coin

1294

New silver mine found at Kutna Hora, Bohemia, which produces 20–25 tons per year. Its silver spreads coin and money use into eastern Europe

14th century

Rise of managed public debts among city-states of northern Italy

Early 15th century

Bullion famine causes shortages of money

Late 15th century

New silver mines found at Schwaz in Tyrol, Schneeberg and Annaberg in Saxony. Portuguese establish direct route to gold supplies in west Africa. The precious metal wealth of the New World begins to flow back to Europe

1512

Large silver mine found in St Joachimsthal in Bohemia. The coins made there, called *thalers*, give their name to the dollar currency unit of later centuries

1545

Huge silver mine found at Potosi in Bolivia. Its silver is transported up the west coast of Latin America, over the Panama isthmus and eastwards to Spain in treasure fleets. Start of the age of Spanish 'pieces of eight' (8-reales pieces), the first trade coin used worldwide; also exported westwards into China via the Philippines

16th century

"Price revolution" – sixfold rise in prices between 1540 and 1640 is probably caused by a huge increase in the quantity of money in circulation

Late 16th–early 17th centuries

Revival of copper coinage throughout Europe. Money use becomes more widespread throughout all levels of society

Late 16th century

Introduction of early mechanised forms of coin production, allowing expansion of coins in circulation and coin use. By 1700 handstriking is obsolete

1566–68

Sir Thomas Gresham builds the Royal Exchange in London as a centre for bankers. He persuades Queen Elizabeth I to reissue the coinage at a higher silver purity; hence his association with Gresham's Law (Bad money drives out good)

1602

Dutch East India Company founded. Trading in its stock and shares lays the basis for modern share dealing

1605

Foundation of Papal Banco de Santo Spirito to provide funds for charitable institutions

1609

Amsterdam Exchange Bank founded. By about 1650 it holds as much capital as the whole of the rest of Europe

1649–60

Commonwealth of England strikes first coins with inscriptions in English

1656

First state bank, Stockholm Banco, founded in Sweden by Johan Palmstruch

1661

First European paper money issued, in Sweden

1692–94

Minas Gerais gold mines found in Brazil, expanding gold supply to Europe

Late 17th century

Spread of public debts among European countries to provide credit for increasingly expensive state-sponsored enterprises, particularly war

1694

Foundation of Bank of England by Act of Parliament as a joint-stock company with limited liability to allow the government to finance its wars in the Netherlands. Notes issued from foundation

1695

Foundation of Bank of Scotland. Notes issued from foundation

1701

First decimal coinage system, in Russia

18th century

Spread of country banks in Britain, many issuing paper notes

1706

Foundation of Vienna Stadt-Banco

1716

Banque Générale founded in Paris by a Scot, John Law; nationalised as the Banque Royale in 1719; bankrupt in 1720

1776

Adam Smith writes *An Inquiry into the Nature and Causes of the Wealth of Nations,* promulgating the Labour Theory of Value, arguing that a nation's wealth is measured "first, by the skill, dexterity and judgement with which its labour is generally applied; and, secondly, by the proportion between the number of those who are employed in useful labour, and that of those who are not so employed".

1789

French revolutionary government begins issue of paper *assignats*, initially treasury bonds but quickly circulating as money. Over-issue undermines their value

1797

Re-establishment of copper token coinage in issue after long period of intermission

1797–1821

The "Restriction Period" in Britain. Paper money is rendered inconvertible against coin throughout the Napoleonic war period

1800

Napoleon founds Banque de France

1810

Royal Mint moves from Tower of London to new building on Tower Hill

1817

Gold sovereign coin introduced in Britain with St George and Dragon design by Benedetto Pistrucci. Still in use today

1817

David Ricardo writes an important treatise, *The Principles of Political Economy and Taxation*, stating: "There is no point more important in issuing paper money than to be fully impressed with the effects that follow from the principle of limitation of quantity. It is not necessary that paper should be payable in specie to secure its value, it is only necessary that its quantity should be regulated."

1840s–50s

New gold mines discovered in Australia and California, encouraging the spread of the international gold standard throughout Europe in later 19th century

1865

Foundation of Latin Monetary Union, a coinage union which grew to include France, Belgium, Switzerland, Italy, Greece. Eventually abolished in 1914

1867–94

Publication of Karl Marx's *Das Kapital*, a fundamental critique of the capitalist system, predicting its inevitable self-destruction

1873

Gold mark replaces thaler as basic German monetary unit

1880s

Discovery of gold in South Africa

1914–18

First world war

1922–23

Period of hyper-inflation in post-war Germany

1925

Winston Churchill as chancellor takes Britain

back on to the international gold standard. All European countries are back on it by 1928

1929

The Wall Street Crash, cause of the Great Depression of the 1930s

1931

Britain suspends payments in gold and comes off the international gold standard

1936

J.M. Keynes publishes *The General Theory of Employment, Interest and Money*, arguing the virtues of government deficit spending as a stimulus to demand in order to release economies from recession

1939–45

Second world war

1947

All silver removed from British coinage

1957

European Economic Community founded by Treaty of Rome

1958

West European currencies fully convertible for first time since second world war

1967

Devaluation of sterling; Royal Mint moves from Tower Hill to Llantrisant, South Wales

1971

British currency decimalised

1999

Euro currency introduced in most countries of the European Union

The Americas

AD

11th century

Viking settlers take coins to America

16th century

Spanish settlers in Mexico report the use of copper axe-ingots as a means of payment

16th–17th centuries

European colonists describe the use of shells

woven into belts as money

1652

First silver coins struck in North America in Boston by Massachusetts Bay Company

1690

First issue of paper money in America by Massachusetts Bay Company

1775–79

$240 million in paper money (called Continentals) issued to pay costs of American revolution

1791

Foundation of Bank of the United States to provide stable currency and fund the public debt left from the Revolution. Controversy over its legitimacy leads to the formation of the first US political parties – Federalists and Democratic Republicans. Charter not renewed in 1811

1792

Dollar adopted as principal US denomination for silver coinage

1816

Bank of the United States refounded. Suspended in 1836 after financial scandal

1858

Canada adopts dollar standard and decimal coinage

1861

First issue of US paper money during Civil War

1862–65

US government issues $450 million in paper money not backed by gold. The debate over whether to restrict or expand quantities in circulation divides US politics for the next 20 years

1913

US Federal Reserve founded

1929

The Wall Street Crash, prelude to the Great Depression of the 1930s

1932

President Franklin D. Roosevelt institutes the New Deal to combat the economic and social

effects of the Depression
1933
United States comes off international gold standard
1936
Fort Knox built
1944
Bretton Woods Conference establishes International Bank for Reconstruction and Development and International Monetary Fund to provide capital for post-war development and stabilise international exchange rates
1950
First credit card introduced by Diner's Club
1971
United States severs link between dollar and gold

Oceania

AD
19th century
Travellers observe the use of feathers, cloth, shells and stones as money
1840s
Hawaiian Kingdom issues first independent coinage in tthe Pacific
1850
Gold mines discovered in Australia
1855
Gold sovereigns issued in Australia
1910–11
Australian Commonwealth coinage commences
1933–40
New Zealand coinage commences
1966
Australia adopts dollar
1967
New Zealand adopts dollar
1988
Australia begins to issue plastic banknotes

The oldest coins and banknotes

Lydia and the West

The first coins were made in the kingdom of Lydia in western Asia Minor (Turkey) in the 7th century BC. The Lydians grew wealthy from the alluvial gold they collected in the form of a gold-silver alloy called electrum and from the peoples and cities they ruled, including the Greek communities of the coast. These early coins were simply small, weighed nuggets of metal of variable shape, stamped on either side with an animal symbol and an abstract punch mark.

The earliest coin hoard consisting of electrum coins was found beneath the Temple of Artemis in Ephesus, one of the seven wonders of the Ancient World. It was discovered in 1904–5 during the course of excavations undertaken by the British Museum. It was presumably placed in the foundations of the temple as a votive offering to the goddess.

In the mid-6th century the kingdom was ruled by King Croesus, made famous as the wealthiest man of his time by the Greek historian, Herodotus. During his reign the Lydians began to make pure gold and silver coins. He was overthrown by the Persians in 547BC.

The Chinese tradition

At almost the same time coins began to be made in the various kingdoms of ancient China. They were cast bronze rather than struck precious metal and were anything but round. The earliest coins, in the shape of knives and small spades, were made in the Zhou kingdom in the late 7th or early 6th century BC.

Within three centuries all the other Chinese kingdoms had started to make coins. Spade-shaped coins were the most popular, but there were a number of different forms. The Chu kingdom's coins were bronze cowrie shells; the Qi state's coins resembled knives; and the coins of the Wei kingdom were round with a hole in the centre. These provided the model for traditional Chinese coinage until the end of the 19th century.

Banknotes in China and the East

The earliest forms of paper money were authorised in Song Dynasty China (960–1279). They were produced to facilitate inter-regional trade in a period of increasing prosperity and expanding commerce within a huge country which otherwise used only low-value bronze or iron coins. At first they were exchange, remittance or credit notes with a date limitation.

In 1189, under the Jin dynasty (1115–1234), exchange certificates with no date limitation were issued. This was the first real paper money in free circulation. The Mongol Yuan dynasty (1206–1367) forbade the use of coins and allowed only paper money to circulate. Marco Polo commented on the strange custom of the use of paper for money in late 13th century China:

> When these papers have been so long in circulation that they are growing torn and frayed, they are brought to the mint and changed for new and fresh ones at a discount of 3%. If a man wants to buy gold or silver ... he goes to the Khan's mint with some of these papers and gives them in payment ... All the Khan's armies are paid with this sort of money.

The earliest bank notes in Europe

Sweden issued the earliest paper money in Europe. In 1656 the Livonian Johan Palmstruch founded the Stockholm Banco as a private institution with responsibility for managing the state's financial affairs. Sweden was rich in copper resources. To maintain the price of copper in world markets it introduced a non-token copper coinage to replace silver. The massive copper plates which resulted from this policy were heavy and inconvenient, so in 1661 Palmstruch hit on the idea of issuing paper credit notes as an alternative currency. Within a few years, however, the bank had issued too many notes and found it could no longer redeem them. In 1667 Palmstruch was accused of mismanagement and condemned to death. The sentence was later commuted.

Why coinage was invented

Herodotus, the "Father of History" (c. 484–425BC), was the first author to speculate on the origins of coinage. He correctly located them in the Kingdom of Lydia in western Turkey, saying that "the Lydians were the first men we know of to strike coins (*nomismata*) of gold and silver, and they were the first to be involved in retail trade". Herodotus seems to have imagined that coins were invented to faciliate buying and selling in the market place. They were certainly used for this purpose in the cosmopolitan imperial city of Athens where Herodotus lived, but the earliest Lydian and Greek coins were large, high-value pieces of silver and electrum, of no use for small-scale retail transactions.

The Greek philosopher Aristotle (384–322BC) wrote more theoretically about the evolution of coinage from primitive systems of trade, and about coinage as a universal medium of exchange. In the *Nichomachean Ethics* he wrote: "All things which can be exchanged need to be compared. For this purpose coinage has come into being, and is a sort of medium." He explained the use of gold and silver coinage as a social convention, relating the Greek word for coin (*nomisma*) to the word for custom (*nomos*). Coinage, he argued, allowed the value of all things to be measured against one another. This possibility of commensurability between different sorts of goods and services allows for exchange between different sorts of people, which in turn promotes the growth of political association among different groups. Aristotle's ideas about the social effects of exchange and money find echoes in the writings of many modern economic thinkers.

In his *Politics* Aristotle sketches out a schema for the historical development of coinage. When human communities began to diversify, they needed to exchange things with other groups to secure their needs. This was a form of natural exchange, not aimed at profit, which led to the growth of import and export for profit. Iron, silver and other similar materials were initially fixed on as a general medium of exchange because they were portable and useful in themselves. At first they were defined merely by size and weight. Then they were stamped (made into coins) to save them from having to be weighed, the stamp being a sign of value. Only then, Aristotle argues, did small-scale retail trade come about.

Why then did the Greeks take to coinage so readily in the 6th century BC? What were its advantages compared with weighed silver bullion, which had been in use for at least two millennia? One possibility is that it allowed the state to make a profit on the minting process by overvaluing the silver minted in its name as coin relative to its bullion value. It is likely that in the city-states of ancient Greece, at least, coinage caught on initially as an official instrument to facilitate the making of state payments, rather than as a response to economic demand or to encourage long-distance trade and the domestic economy. This was why it took so long for most Greek states to issue low-value base-metal coins. Though the Greek cities of Sicily began making bronze coins in the fifth-century BC, they did not catch on in Athens, the major coin-producing city of ancient Greece, until the late fourth century. Until then, the Athenians made tiny silver coins for use as loose change. They were small enough to be carried around in the mouth. The striking of bullion as coin also made money a countable and therefore more tractable substance, compared with weighing out the bullion required for every new transaction.

Greek city-states were also intensely competitive in their relations with one another. If one major city had a successful coinage, there would have been a natural tendency for its rivals to acquire one for themselves. As coinage was made of precious metal, they could be traded as a commodity as well as being used as a means of exchange. Athenian silver coins were traded all over the eastern Mediterranean and widely copied from Asia Minor to Egypt in the fifth and fourth centuries BC.

Ancient and medieval ideas about coinage

The Greeks

The Greek philosophers were concerned about the moral and practical effects of the use of gold and silver as money. In Plato's *Republic*, Socrates argues that the guardians of his ideal state should not use gold or silver or even come into contact with it "since there is much evil caused by the coinage used by the people". One of the characters in Plato's philosophical dialogue, the *Laws*, goes further, saying that no citizens should be allowed to possess gold or silver in the ideal state, and that they should use coinage only for daily transactions. This coinage must not be current beyond the boundaries of the state, to prevent the evils of long-distance trade and acquisitiveness. The philosophical strictures of Plato found a historical parallel in the militaristic city-state of Sparta, where there seems to have been a law, or at least a strong moral prohibition, against the possession of gold and silver by citizens. Instead, Spartans may have used iron spits as currency which were indeed worthless beyond their borders. Plato was perhaps inspired by the Spartan example.

Aristotle also worried about the fixation on metal as money. In the *Politics* he wrote: "Coinage sometimes seems to be a nonsense and pure convention, with no real existence in nature. For if those who use it change it, it is worth nothing and not useful for any of the necessities of life."

Ancient China

The earliest recorded speculations on the origins of coinage in ancient China are attributed to a Chinese minister who died in 645BC, in the *Book of Master Guan*, written around 26BC: "The early kings put a value on things from the furthest distance that were difficult to find. They saw pearls and jade as superior money, gold as medium money, and spades and knives [the shapes of the earliest Chinese coins] as inferior money. You cannot wear money but you can be warm; you cannot eat money, but you can fill your belly. The early kings amassed stores of wealth with which they ruled the people, thereby bringing peace to the world."

Like the Greeks, Chinese authors also worried about the moral effects of coinage: "Since the appearance of the wuzhu coins over 70 years ago, many people have been found guilty of illicit coining. The rich hoard housefuls of coins, and yet are never satisfied. The people are restless. The merchants seek profit. Though you give land to the poor people, they must still sell cheaply to the merchant. They become poorer and poorer, then become bandits. The reason? It is the deepening of the secondary occupations and the coveting of money. That is why evil cannot be banned. It arises entirely out of money." (Gong Yu, c. 45BC)

Islam and Christianity

The early Islamic community (7th century AD) used coinage, imitating Byzantine gold and copper coinage in the west and Sasanian (Persian) silver coinage in the east. But the Prophet Muhammad was aware of the moral problems associated with money – he had been a merchant before receiving his call. Two sayings attributed to him are: "There are two hungry wolves in our society – money and status" and "Money puts my community to the test". Usury, that is lending money at interest, was forbidden by the *Qur'an*, as it was by Jesus in the Sermon on the Mount.

Christianity also had (and has) moral problems with the power of money, which it inherited from Judaism. "The judgements of the Lord are true and righteous altogether. Much more to be desired are they than gold, more than much fine gold," says the psalmist.

St Paul wrote "Love of money is the root of all evil". This is often misquoted as "Money is the root of all evil". But greed, not money itself, was his target.

The medieval world

Medieval European theologians and philosophers speculated on the origins, nature and operations of money. St Thomas Aquinas (1225–74) wrote about the problem of the "just price" of goods and services: "It is wholly sinful to practise fraud for the purpose of selling a thing for more than its just price. To sell dearer or buy cheaper than a thing is worth is in itself unjust and unlawful." How to establish what the just price should be was left unclear. However, St Thomas would not have referred the matter to the free market, a concept which was opposed to his notions of divine justice. He approved of trade and exchange which provided for the necessities of life, but condemned all forms of trade and monetary exchange purely for the pursuit of gain and more money. In other words, money should not be used to make money. This was closely bound up with the traditional Christian prohibition on usury which was regarded as unnatural.

Nicholas Oresme (c. 1320–82), bishop of Lisieux, was perhaps the next most important medieval monetary thinker. He wrote a treatise *On the Origin, Nature, Law and Alterations of Money*: "Men were subtle enough to devise the use of money to be the instrument of natural riches which of themselves minister to human need … For money does not directly relieve the necessities of life, but is an instrument artificially invented for the easier exchange of natural riches. And it is clear without further proof that coin is very useful to the civil community, and convenient, or rather necessary, to the business of the state." Nicholas was more open than St Thomas to the business of mercantile trade, but he too was opposed to lending money at interest: "There are three ways in which profit may be made from money without laying it out for its natural purpose (ie, buying the necessities of life): one is the art of the money-changer, banking or exchange; another is usury; a third is the alteration (ie, debasement) of coinage. The first way is contemptible, the second bad, the third worse."

Biggest, rarest, most valuable

Ancient coins are not necessarily worth more at auction than more modern pieces. The prices realised depend on the health of the market rather than on the age or even the rarity of the coin. The highest prices are generally obtained on the American coin market, where there are many collectors with substantial disposable income. American collectors also tend to prefer collecting US coins, the rarest of which can sell for large sums.

In 1996 a dealer paid $1,485,000 for a rare 1913 Liberty nickel coin, one of only five known to exist. At the time this was the highest price paid for an American coin at auction (another one of the five had sold for $962,500 in 1993). However, in 1997 a collector paid $1,815,000 for an 1804 silver dollar, the "king of American coins". Also in 1996, a Roman gold coin of the usurper emperor Saturninus sold in London for £264,000. While six years earlier a unique gold coin made by Brutus, the murderer of Julius Caesar, in 44BC sold for $550,000. However, in 1980, a silver decadrachma of the city of Acragas in Sicily made $572,000. Taking inflation into account, this is the highest price ever realised for an ancient coin. Also in 1996 in the United States a 1907 $20 gold coin was sold for $825,000, a record price for a gold coin. In 1995 a Spanish gold coin made in Seville between 1469 and 1504 sold for $364,550, reportedly the highest price realised for a medieval coin. In 1999 the comparatively small sum of £4,200 was paid for a unique Ancient British coin at auction in London. Yet this was reportedly the highest price ever paid for such a coin at auction.

Banknotes do not generally fetch such high prices, but six-figure sums have been paid. Rarity, serial number and condition are important in determining the value of a note. For example, a 1937–40 Mauritian 1,000 rupee note with the number A0000 sold at auction in London for £17,250, and a rare 1924 Australian £1,000 note sold in Melbourne for A$86,000. In 1998 $126,000 was paid for a 1928 $10,000 Federal Reserve note, a record for small-size American notes. High denomination notes are usually made in the lowest quantities and are thus generally rarer.

Biggest banknotes

Ever since their introduction banknotes have remained more or less the same size as they are now, with larger denominations tending to be somewhat larger. However, in the 19th century notes were certainly larger than the current standard, sometimes up to twice the size. The largest banknotes ever to have been in general circulation are probably Chinese notes of the Ming dynasty: 1,000 cash notes made in the Hungwu reign (1368–98) measured 10 inches by 16 inches (26cm x 40cm). By contrast, the large "white fivers", the old British £5 notes sometimes seen in films of the 1940s and 1950s, which seem so large to modern-day viewers, measured only 8.25 by 5 inches (21cm x 13cm).

Largest denomination coins...

The earliest Lydian and Greek coins were of a high denomination, being made of electrum, a naturally occurring alloy of gold and silver, and large pieces of silver sometimes weighing up to 8 drachmas (32g). These coins were not intended for everyday use.

The highest denomination coin (in real terms) ever made was probably the Mughal emperor Jahangir's 1,000 mohur gold coin (1613), a large gold presentation piece weighing almost 11kg. In more recent times, an emergency issue of coins in the German state of Westphalia in 1923 included a coin with the value of 1 billion marks, and in 1946 Romania issued a silver coin with a face value of Lei100,000. Modern gold coins can often reach high denominational values. In 1970 Chad issued a Fr20,000 gold piece, and in the same year South Korea issued a W25,000 gold coin weighing almost 1kg. In 1975 Laos produced a K100,000 coin. In 1990 Greece issued a Dr20,000 coin to celebrate the 50th anniversary of the Italian invasion. These coins are not for everyday circulation and are often made in small quantities for collectors. Only 1,000 of the Greek coins were produced, for example. Of course, high denominations do not necessary mean high values.

...and banknotes

In the modern world the effects of hyperinflation have produced some remarkably high denomination banknotes. In the early 1920s Germany produced banknotes in increasingly large numbers and of ever higher values. In 1922 notes of thousands of marks became common, and in 1923 they passed 1m and reached 1 milliard (1,000m). In 1924 notes to the value of 1m million marks were produced. The record for the highest denomination banknote ever produced belongs to Hungary, which in 1946 made a note to the value of 100m billion pengo. In Greece in 1944 banknotes of Dr2,000m, Dr10,000m and Dr100,000m were produced.

More recently, the new states of eastern Europe and the Balkans have indulged in inflationary over-production of paper money. The paper currency of the breakaway Serb Republic in Bosnia quickly descended from sensible denominations of YuD10, YuD50 and YuD100 in 1992 to YuD50m, YuD100m and YuD500m in 1993. In Serbia itself in 1993 notes to the value of YuD500,000m were produced. A currency reform in 1994 rendered 1 new dinar equal to 1,000m old dinars.

Rarest old coins...

Many issues of coin from the ancient world of Greece and Rome are rare, not necessarily because they were made in small quantities but simply because few have survived the accidents of history. Paradoxically, therefore, unique coins are not that unusual. One of the most important, now in the British Museum, is a coin of Octavian (later to become the emperor Augustus) of 28BC, the year when he claimed to be restoring the Roman Republic after 20 years of arbitrary rule and civil war, but was actually establishing himself as monarch. The inscription on the back reads, disingenuously, "He has restored to the People of Rome their laws and rights". Another unique coin of Augustus of 12BC shows the emperor raising a personification of the Roman Republic from her knees – the emperor as saviour of the state.

The usurper Roman emperor Silbannacus (mid-3rd century AD) is known to history solely because of the two surviving coins in his name. He is not mentioned in any ancient source.

There is only one coin extant from medieval Wales, made at Chester for a Welsh prince, Hywel Dda (died 949), also in the British Museum.

In the modern world, among the most famous of rare coins is the 1933 British penny, of which only seven examples are known. In 1994 one was sold at auction for £20,000. News of this sale spread throughout the world, exciting the hopes of many who found that they had pennies from 1932 or 1934, years when several million pennies were made. But this cannot compare with the almost $1.5m paid in 1996 for one of the five known 1913 US Liberty nickels.

...and banknotes

Paper money, because of the material from which it is made, has less chance of surviving hundreds, let alone thousands, of years. However, paper money has often been mass-produced in huge quantities and certain notes of some historical periods, such as the American Civil War (1861–65), are still freely available. An extremely rare 1797 Bank of England £1 note, by contrast, was sold at auction for £52,000. British banknotes from the 19th and early 20th centuries, particularly in high denominations (£200, £500, £1,000), are often rare and can fetch high prices at auction. The same is true for American high denomination notes ($500, $1,000) of the same period. There is, for instance, only one known example of the 1891 $1,000 note, and all legal tender issues of 1869 are famously rare. From an earlier period, 14th-century Chinese paper money from the Ming dynasty (1368–1644) is, perhaps understandably given its age, also rare.

Making and unmaking money

Today coins and banknotes that are legal tender are prescribed by law and foreign or outdated currency is kept out of circulation by banks and retailers. In the past governments and merchants often took a more relaxed attitude towards alien or non-legal currencies. This was partly because precious metal coinage has an intrinsic value however old it is or wherever it comes from, and partly because the official systems of control were weak and not centralised.

Coins can last in circulation for a long time. Before decimalisation came in in the UK in 1971 there were even some Roman bronze *sestertii* in circulation as pennies. Governments can decide to demonetise a particular sort of coin for economic or political reasons. The Romans demonetised the silver coins made by the Italians in their rebellion against Roman domination in the 80s BC. Consequently, only 900 or so coins of the many thousands originally made by the Italians survive today. Similarly, the Commonwealth coinage was demonetised by the restored monarchy in England in 1660, primarily for political reasons.

In a world where coinage is made of gold and silver, of course, money has an intrinsic value, which remains potentially valid across political barriers. There is also a strong financial disincentive against bearing the costs associated with withdrawing a particular coinage, reminting and reissuing it as legal tender. To avoid such costs, a monetary authority may try simply to strike new designs over the top of an existing coinage without melting it down. The Jewish rebels against the Romans in the 130s AD produced their own coinage in this way.

Precious-metal coins can be driven out of circulation by the introduction of new, debased coins with a lower gold or silver content. If two groups of coins have the same face value but contain different quantities of precious metal, the poorer-quality coins will tend to drive the better ones out of circulation as they are hoarded or sold as bullion by the coin-using population. This general monetary law, that "bad money drives out good", is particularly associated with the name of Sir Thomas Gresham (1519–79), English merchant and financier who founded the Royal Exchange in London.

The market usually sufficed as a mechanism to remove better money in the advent of worse. But sometimes older, purer coins were deliberately removed from circulation through government action. Over the first two centuries AD, the Roman emperors were unable to resist reducing the silver content of the *denarius* in order to make their silver supplies go further in monetary terms and fund their ever-increasing deficits. The emperor Trajan (AD 98–117) demonetised all the old, nearly pure silver coins from the Republican period in order to make more, debased coins supposedly worth the same but containing substantially less silver.

Where money is represented by materials of purely token value, it is only a law or custom that gives the coin or note a monetary worth. So there is no place in modern national currency systems for coins from former times or other countries unless they fit in with the new denominational system, as did various British pre-decimal coins made as long ago as 1948 until 1990. The motor behind the demonetisation of a modern coinage is often the need to replace it with a cheaper, more durable or more secure alternative which uses up less metal, or is made of a more cost-effective material or is less liable to forgery. Coins declared to be no longer legal tender are quickly withdrawn from circulation by banks and returned to the mint for recycling as new coinage. A 1995 survey found that loss rates for coins in the UK varied from 3.5% a year for the 1 penny coin (of a total of 6,400m circulation) to 0.8% a year for the 50 pence coin (of a total of 480m in circulation). There were 17,300m coins in circulation with a total value of nearly £2 billion.

Despite the fact that non-cash transactions make up an increasing proportion of total transactions, world demand for coins still increases annually. In 1993–94 the British Royal Mint, which makes coins for 70 different countries, reported that it had produced 21% more coins for circulation in the UK (a total of 1,366m) than in 1992–93. Yet in the same year the total value of coins in circulation was only one-tenth of notes and one-300th of the total money supply (M4).

Banknotes, unlike coinage, do not last long when in continuous circulation, and they need to be constantly replaced. Until recently, the Bank of England incinerated its disused notes and used the resulting energy to heat its printing works. Now, for environmental reason, notes are shredded and used for landfill. In financial year 1998–9, the Bank of England reported that there were £24.8 billion worth of banknotes in circulation, as opposed to £23.5 billion in the preceding financial year.

According to the European Monetary Institute, at the end of 1996 there were 12.7 billion banknotes circulating in the countries of the European Union (2,130m in the UK). The estimated average life of a banknote is two years, thus requiring a production level of over 6 billion notes a year just to keep up, let alone meet increased demand. Across the EU as a whole, the ratio of the value of banknotes in circulation to GDP was 5.8%, ranging from 2.4% in Finland to 11% in Spain (3.7% in the UK).

In 1996 coin production in the United States was expected to exceed the 1995 record total production figure of 19.8 billion, and 10 billion notes were expected to be produced by the Bureau of Engraving and Printing. US Mint figures show that in 1998 16.1 billion coins were made for general circulation; in 1997, Bureau of Engraving and Minting figures for banknote production totalled 9.5 billion, with a value of $142 billion. In 1996, up to $140 billion worth of US notes circulated within the United States; a further £250 billion circulated abroad.

Alternative money

Bullion and ingots

Before coins were invented (in the 7th century BC in Asia Minor and China), and in many parts of the world since, metal weighed out as bullion has often been used as money for exchange or for paying taxes or legal fines.

The Babylonian Lawcode of Hammurabi (1792–50BC) stipulates wage rates, fines and interest rates in terms of weighed amounts of silver (in *minas* and *shekels*, the Semitic word for weight). Silver was also used as a standard money of account in ancient Mesopotamia. Grain by volume appears in lawcodes and documentary texts as a means of making payments and expressing the values of various goods and services.

In ancient Egypt the silver standard also seems to have operated. Gold was in use as well, often in the form of rings, and weights of copper bullion (the unit was the *deben*, of 91g) were used to make payments and express the values of other commodities.

In both these societies the existence of a metal standard allowed systems of barter to operate and monetary equivalences to be made between goods of different kinds.

Even among the coin-using Greeks, there were many cities and peoples that did not use coinage. The Spartans had a law against it, and seem to have used iron spits instead. This was a misguided attempt to prevent the moral problems which were thought to come with gold and silver coinage. Spits (*oboloi*, a name also given to a small silver denomination) have been found by archaeologists on temple sites. They seem to have been in use as some form of low-value currency. In Homer, bronze tripods appear to have been a recognised standard of value.

The earliest Roman lawcode, the Twelve Tables (450BC), mentions penal fines assessed in terms of weights (*asses*) of cast bronze. These large cast ingots were used to make payments of various sorts, both legal and monetary.

Julius Caesar, in his accounts of his conquest of Gaul in the 50s BC, and of his two invasions of south-east England in 55BC and 54BC, describes the monetary habits of the ancient Britons, saying that they used iron bars instead of coins. The ancient Britons did use and make coins in gold, silver and bronze, but blunt sword-shaped iron bars have been found by archaeologists. These may be what Caesar describes.

The use of precious-metal bullion as money returned in Late Antiquity and continued into the early Middle Ages.

In the late Roman Empire (4th century AD) emperors would make payments to their troops and other favoured subjects in forms other than traditional coinage. These included precious-metal belt buckles and leaf-shaped pieces of gold and silver, as well as silver and gold plate of various sorts. Silver spoons are often found in coin hoards in Britain from this period, suggesting that they may have had some monetary use.

Shells

Their decorative use in personal adornment has made shells a popular form of money in so-called primitive societies throughout the world. In the 16th century, European travellers in the Congo noted the use of *lumache* shells instead of gold and silver coinage. In 19th-century New Britain, an island north-east of New Guinea, small humped *tambu* shells threaded onto rattan cords were used.

In the 20th century crescent-shaped *kina* shells were used in Papua New Guinea. The modern currency of Papua New Guinea is called the kina after these shells, which were often strung together into impressive banners and used to make various social payments, such as bride prices. They have now been replaced by paper money, but the kina shell still appears as an element in the design on the country's modern banknotes.

The modern world's money is ultimately derived from the precious metal-based moneys of the ancient Near East. But almost as long-lived and widespread a form of money was the cowrie, the shell of a small sea-dwelling snail, about 2.5cm long, from the Indian and Pacific Oceans. In about the 13th century BC cowrie shells are recorded as being used as gifts in China. Some of the earliest bronze Chinese coins were imitations of the cowrie shell (5th–3rd century BC).

Cowries were regularly used as a form of small change in India until the 19th century. In 1780 the British issued a new coinage for British India, establishing an exchange rate of 5,120 cowries to 1 silver rupee. The copper coinage made by the British East India Company was unable to compete in the market with the cowrie and was forced out of production in 1784.

In the 14th century Arab merchants traded cowries in the kingdom of Mali in west Africa, where they came to be widely employed as a means of exchange and personal adornment. Portuguese, British, Dutch and French traders took up the trade, importing huge quantities of cowries into western Africa from the Indian Ocean to trade for slaves. Cowries were also used as currency in India, but the African trade caused a shortage of shells so almonds had to be used there instead.

The cowrie is used as a device on coins of the modern state of Ghana, recalling its former use as the local currency.

Wampum

One of the most famous forms of non-coin money, wampum, or wampumpeag, literally means "strings of white beads". It consisted of either strings or whole belts of clam shells, which were initially used by Native American peoples on the east coast of America for various ceremonial purposes.

In the 17th century European settlers came to use it as a means of exchange with the Native Americans. In the 18th century machine-made wampum was produced in such large amounts that it lost its value and ceased to be used in the eastern part of the country. It continued in use in the West until the mid-19th century.

Salt and rice

Because it is a necessary part of the human diet, salt has been used as a medium of exchange at various times and places. In the 16th century a Portuguese missionary, Francis Alvarez, reported that it was in use from Abyssinia (Ethiopia) to the Congo. In the early 18th century a British merchant, Alexander Hamilton, wrote that salt was used together with various foreign coins as money in Ethiopia: 80 bricks of salt were equivalent to 1 wakea (an Abyssinian ounce) of gold.

Salt was also used as money in peripheral provinces of the Chinese Empire. A 9th-century writer, Fan Chuo, mentioned the use of salt in the western region of Sichuan. Marco Polo also remarked on this in the same area in the 13th century. Large-scale transactions were conducted in gold ingots, but for smaller amounts the Great Khan's agents made salt bricks for currency. In the 14th century an Arab traveller, Ibn Battuta, reported that salt was being used in the west African kingdom of Mali.

Other staple foods such as rice have also been used as money. In Japan taxes were payable in rice until the Meiji restoration in 1868. Grain was often used as a standard of value in ancient Mesopotamia (see above).

Cattle

The Romans thought that cattle constituted the earliest form of money used by their primitive ancestors. This was because the Latin word for money, *pecunia*, was derived from the word for cattle, *pecus* (the English word 'fee' is related to it). In ancient Irish, Indian and Persian legal and religious texts, reference is often made to valuation (of fines or of a man's worth) and payments in terms of cattle.

An inscription from 1st-century AD western India records a payment of 3,000 cattle by a prince to priests for his ritual purification after battle. In India the term *dakshina* (meaning "a cow on the left", or one set aside for the priest) is still used to describe ritual payments made to priests.

Cloth

Rolls of silk were sometimes used as a means of payment and a measure of value in East Asia. During the Tang Dynasty (618–907) the monetary standard of China was based on silk as well as coinage. One of the most famous of ethnographic studies, by Mary Douglas of the Lele people in Congo, looked at the quasi-monetary circulation of raffia cloths among the Lele in the early 1950s. These cloths were used to make various social and religious payments, and their circulation was controlled by the tribal elders. They acted as a form of social control. But when younger Lele began to earn money in the colonial economy and were paid in coins and banknotes, they bought cloths with the money and thus upset the delicate social balance maintained by the cloth system.

Ingots in South-East Asia

In Malaysia and Indonesia ingots of tin in various curious shapes, including hats, crocodiles and cockerels, were used as money. Reports from Chinese writers mention their use in the 15th century. In Borneo, indigenous peoples used small bronze imitation cannon as a form of money. In Burma and Thailand silver ingots, shaped like snail-shells, canoes, bent rings and spheres, circulated until the 19th century.

Cigarettes and tobacco

In Germany after the second world war, a barter economy prevailed in which one of the most widely used forms of currency was cigarettes. Tobacco was also used by various Native American peoples as a form of money.

Stamps

In France, Germany and other countries in Europe after the first world war stamps of the required denomination, mounted in small metal discs, circulated as money in place of coins. This practice has occurred in various parts of the world in times of currency shortage and originated in America during the Civil War (1861–65).

Buried treasure

Coin hoards are vital for the understanding of monetary history as well as coinage. They provide new raw material and evidence of previously unknown types of coin, and they show what kinds of coin were in circulation and being hoarded at a particular time. Coins have been hoarded (buried in the ground) for various reasons: as a basic means of safe-keeping in periods of disturbance, especially before the advent of savings banks; or perhaps as monetary offerings to a divinity.

It is not unlikely that large coin hoards are regularly found around the world which are dispersed before being properly recorded. The numbers of coins in precious metal coin hoards are most often in the tens or hundreds, some in the thousands and a very few in the hundreds of thousands. This is because most hoards represent the personal wealth not of the richest in society, who would have other ways of securing their wealth, but of people with some substantial wealth worth concealing but small enough in quantity to be hoarded in one or two pots or boxes in a field somewhere. There are rumours that massive hoards of Bactrian Greek coins, consisting of hundreds of thousands of coins, have been found in Afghanistan, but these cannot be confirmed.

Record funds

The largest hoards are often of Roman coins. The largest recorded was found in Reka Devnia (ancient Marcianopolis) in Bulgaria and consisted of 81,000 silver denarii. It is likely that this was not the whole find – estimates of the residue range from 20,000 to 160,000. Two of the largest coin hoards have been found in the UK. In 1978, 54,951 base-silver Roman coins of the 3rd century AD were found at Mildenhall (ancient Cunetio) in Wiltshire. They were acquired by the British Museum for further study. In 1988, 47,909 Roman coins of the same period were discovered at Normanby in Lincolnshire. In 1992 the famous Hoxne hoard of 4th-century AD Roman gold and silver coins was found in Suffolk. It consisted of 15,000 coins and 200 assorted other gold and silver objects, including spoons, dishes and bracelets. The hoard was acquired intact by the British Museum. Coins are hoarded whenever and wherever they appear. In north-west China a massive hoard of 45kg of bronze *wuzhu* coins (118BC–621AD) has been unearthed.

PART 2

THE WORLD
OF MONEY

Who uses what

Country	Currency	Symbol
Afghanistan	afghani	Af
Albania	lek	Lk
Algeria	New (Algerian) dinar	AD
Angola	readjusted kwanza	Kzr
Argentina	peso	Ps
Armenia	dram	Dram
Aruba	Aruban florin	Afl
Australia	Australian dollar	A$
Austria	schilling	ASch
Azerbaijan	manat	Manat
Bahamas	Bahamian dollar	B$
Bahrain	Bahraini dinar	BD
Bangladesh	taka	Tk
Barbados	Barbados dollar	Bds $
Belarus	Belarusian rouble	BRb
Belgium	Belgian franc	Bfr
Belize	Belize dollar	Bz$
Benin	CFA franc	CFAfr
Bermuda	Bermuda dollar	Bda$
Bhutan	ngultrum	Nu
Bolivia	boliviano	Bs
Bosnia	convertible marka	KM
Botswana	pula	P
Brazil	real	R
Brunei	Brunei dollar/ringgit	Br$
Bulgaria	lev	Lv
Burkina Faso	CFA franc	CFAfr
Burundi	Burundi franc	Bufr
Cambodia	riel	CR
Cameroon	CFA franc	CFAfr
Canada	Canadian dollar	C$
Cape Verde	Cape Verde escudo	CVEsc

Country	Currency	Symbol
Central African Republic	CFA franc	CFAfr
Chad	CFA franc	CFAfr
Chile	Chilean peso	Ps
China	renminbi	Rmb
Colombia	Colombian peso	Ps
Comoros	Comorian franc	Cfr
Congo (Brazzaville)	CFA franc	CFAfr
Congo (Democratic Rep of)	Congolese franc	FC
Costa Rica	Costa Rican colón	C
Côte d'Ivoire	CFA franc	CFAfr
Croatia	kuna	HRK
Cuba	Cuban peso	Ps
Cyprus	Cyprus pound/Turkish lira	C£/TL
Czech Republic	koruna	Kc
Denmark	Danish krone	DKr
Djibouti	Djibouti franc	Dfr
Dominican Republic	Dominican peso	Ps
Dubai	UAE dirham	Dh
Ecuador	sucre	Su
Egypt	Egyptian pound	£E
El Salvador	El Salvador colón	c
Equatorial Guinea	CFA franc	CFAfr
Eritrea	nafka	Nfa
Estonia	kroon	EEK
Ethiopia	birr	Birr
European Union[a]	euro	€
Fiji	Fiji dollar	F$
Finland	markka	FM
France	franc	FFr

Country	Currency	Symbol
Gabon	CFA franc	CFAfr
The Gambia	dalasi	D
Georgia	lari	Lari
Germany	D-mark	DM
Ghana	cedi	C
Greece	drachma	Dr
Grenada	East Caribbean dollar	EC$
Guatemala	quetzal	Q
Guinea	Guinea franc	Gnf
Guinea-Bissau	CFA franc	CFAfr
Guyana	Guyanese dollar	G$
Haiti	gourde	G
Honduras	lempira	La
Hong Kong	Hong Kong dollar	HK$
Hungary	forint	Ft
Iceland	Iceland new króna	Ikr
India	Indian rupee	Rs
Indonesia	rupiah	Rp
Iran	rial	IR
Iraq	Iraqi dinar	ID
Ireland	punt	IR£
Israel	new Israeli shekel	NIS
Italy	lira (pl. lire)	L
Jamaica	Jamaican dollar	J$
Japan	yen	¥
Jordan	Jordan dinar	JD
Kazakhstan	tenge	Tenge
Kenya	Kenya shilling	KSh
Kirgizstan	som	Som
North Korea	North Korean won	Won
South Korea	South Korean won	W
Kuwait	Kuwaiti dinar	KD
Laos	kip	K
Latvia	lat	LVL
Lebanon	Lebanese pound	L£

Country	Currency	Symbol
Lesotho	loti (pl. maloti)	M
Liberia	Liberian dollar	L$
Libya	Libyan dinar	LD
Lithuania	litis	LTL
Luxembourg	Luxembourg franc	Lfr
Macau	pataca	MPtc
Macedonia	Macedonian dinar	Den
Malagasy	Malagasy franc	Mgfr
Malawi	kwacha	MK
Malaysia	Malaysian dollar/ringgit	M$
Mali	CFA franc	CFAfr
Malta	Maltese lira	Lm
Mauritania	ouguiya	UM
Mauritius	Mauritius rupee	MRs
Mexico	Mexican peso	Ps
Moldova	Moldavian leu (pl. lei)	Lei
Mongolia	togrog	Tg
Morocco	dirham	Dh
Mozambique	metical	MT
Myanmar	kyat	Kt
Namibia	Namibia dollar	N$
Nepal	Nepalese rupee	NRs
Netherlands	guilder	G
Netherlands Antilles	Netherlands Antilles guilder	NAG
New Caledonia	French Pacific franc	CFPfr
New Zealand	New Zealand dollar	NZ$
Nicaragua	córdoba	C
Niger	CFA franc	CFAfr
Nigeria	naira	N
Norway	Norwegian krone	NKr
Oman	Omani rial	OR
Pakistan	Pakistan rupee	PRs
Panama	balboa	B

Country	Currency	Symbol
Papua New Guinea	kina	Kina
Paraguay	guarani	G
Peru	nuevo sol	Ns
Philippines	Philippine peso	P
Poland	zloty (pl. zlotys)	Zl
Portugal	escudo	Esc
Puerto Rico	US dollar	$
Qatar	Qatari riyal	QR
Romania	leu (pl. lei)	Lei
Russia	rouble	Rb
Rwanda	Rwandan franc	Rwfr
São Tomé & Príncipe	dobra	Db
Saudi Arabia	Saudi riyal	SR
Senegal	CFA franc	CFAfr
Serbia-Montenegro	Yugoslav dinar	YuD
Seychelles	Seychelles rupee	SRs
Sierra Leone	leone	Le
Singapore	Singapore dollar	S$
Slovakia	Slovak koruna	Kcs
Slovenia	tolar	SIT
Solomon Islands	Solomon Islands dollar	SI$
Somalia	Somali shilling	SoSh
South Africa	rand	R
Spain	peseta	Pta
Sri Lanka	Sri Lanka rupee	SLRs
Sudan	Sudanese pound/dinar	S£/SD
Suriname	Suriname guilder	SG
Swaziland	lilangeni (pl. emalengeni)	E
Sweden	Swedish krona	SKr
Switzerland	Swiss franc	SFr
Syria	Syrian pound	S£

Country	Currency	Symbol
Taiwan	New Taiwan dollar	NT$
Tanzania	Tanzanian shilling	TSh
Thailand	baht	Bt
Togo	CFA franc	CFAfr
Trinidad & Tobago	Trinidad & Tobago dollar	TT$
Tunisia	Tunisian dinar	TD
Turkey	Turkish lira	TL
Turkmenistan	manat	Manat
Uganda	New Ugandan shilling	NUSh
Ukraine	hryvnya	HRN
United Arab Emirates	UAE dirham	Dh
United Kingdom	pound/sterling	£
United States	dollar	$
Uruguay	Uruguayan new peso	Ps
Uzbekistan	som	Som
Vanuatu	vatu	Vt
Venezuela	bolívar	Bs
Vietnam	dong	D
Western Samoa	tala	Tala
Windward & Leeward Islands[b]	East Caribbean dollar	EC$
Yemen	Yemeni rial	YR
Yugoslavia (Serbia-Montenegro)	Yugoslav dinar	YuD
Zambia	kwacha	ZK
Zimbabwe	Zimbabwe dollar	Z$

a The 11 Eurozone countries that adopted the euro in 1999 are Austria, Belgium, Finland, France, Germany, Ireland, Italy, Luxembourg, Netherlands, Portugal, Spain.
b Antigua & Barbuda, Dominica, Grenada, Monserrat, St Kitts-Nevis, St Lucia, St Vincent & Grenadines, the British Virgin islands.

The Euro

What's to happen when

In place or under way since January 1st 1999
Conversion rates irrevocably fixed; responsibility
of Council (based on Commission proposal)

Single monetary policy in euro; responsibility of
European System of Central Banks

Foreign exchange operations in euro; responsibility
of European System of Central Banks

Public debt issues in euro, some outstanding
debt redenominated in euro; responsibility of
member states, European Investment Bank,
Commission and other issuers

Many large companies begin issuing invoices and
making payments in euro; responsibility of
member states, European Investment Bank,
Commission and other issuers

Banks begin converting payments in national
currency units into euro for euro accounts;
responsibility of member states, European
Investment Bank, Commission and other issuers

Change-over to the euro by the banking and
finance industry

Preparation for orderly change-over of eg, IT,
accounting, dual display of prices etc;
responsibility of Commission and member states

Information campaigns; responsibility of
Commission and member states

January 1st 2002
Start circulation of euro banknotes and coins;
responsibility of European System of Central
Banks

Change-over to the euro of public administrations;
responsibility of member states

July 1st 2002 at the latest
Cancel the legal tender status of national
banknotes and coins; responsibility of
member states, European System of Central
Banks

Fixed conversion rates for participants

Dec 31st 1998
1 euro =

Belgian franc	40.3399	Luxembourg franc	40.3399
German mark	1.95583	Dutch guilder	2.20371
Spanish peseta	166.386	Austrian schilling	13.7603
French franc	6.55957	Portuguese escudo	200.482
Irish punt	0.787564	Finnish markka	5.94573
Italian lira	1936.27		

A bumpy start

1 euro =	Sterling	Swedish krone	Danish krone	Greek drachma	US dollar
1999					
Jan 1st	0.71	9.52	7.47	329	1.17
Jun 1st	0.65	8.98	7.43	324	1.05
Dec 1st	0.63	8.62	7.44	329	1.01
2000					
Jan 1st	0.63	8.57	7.44	330	1.02
June 1st	0.62	8.34	7.47	337	0.93

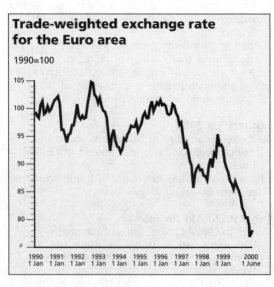

Trade-weighted exchange rate for the Euro area

1990=100

PART 3

HOW MUCH MONEY?

Money supply and control

Money is anything which is accepted as a medium of exchange; essentially currency in circulation plus bank deposits. Notes and coin, issued by the monetary authorities (mainly central banks), account for only a tiny proportion of the money supply. The rest is bank deposits which are initially created within the banking sector.

The total amount of money in circulation, the money stock or money supply depending how you look at it, is often called M. The number of times it changes hands each year is its velocity of circulation, V.

Multiply the two together (M × V) and you have the amount of money that is spent, which by definition must equal real output Y multiplied by the price index P; that is, $M \times V = Y \times P$.

This equation is the basis for understanding money. Assume for the moment that velocity is fixed or predictable (it is not particularly). In this case, argue the monetarists, controlling the money supply controls money GDP (that is, Y × P); and if the trend in real output Y can be predicted inflation can be controlled. Their opponents argue that cause and effect run in the other direction, that money GDP fixes the demand for money and there is nothing that can be done about it.

Whoever is right, if you are prepared to accept that velocity is fixed in the short term, then as a dangerously crude rule of thumb, subtract the inflation rate from the rate of growth of money to estimate the growth of real output.

Money defined

Narrow money, M1. In most countries the measure of narrow money is called M1. This is fairly uniformly defined as currency in circulation plus sight deposits (accounts where cash is available on demand).

There are some national variations. Britain's narrow money measure is called M0. This consists almost entirely of cash in circulation, but also includes banks' operational deposits at the Bank of England. Britain has no M1 measure. America's M1 measure includes traveller's cheques. Japan's definition includes the government's sight deposits.

The number of national variations was reduced in the run-up to the creation of the euro, with the harmonisation of the definition of monetary aggregates across the Eurozone. The European Central Bank publishes monetary statistics for the whole Eurozone from figures compiled by national central banks.

Broad money, M2. The main wider definitions of money are called M2 and M3. In essence, M2 consists of M1 plus savings deposits and time deposits (accounts where cash is available after a notice period). The definition of M3 is wider still.

- In America M2 consists of M1 plus savings deposits, time deposits and retail money-market mutual funds.
- In the Eurozone M2 is defined as M1 plus deposits with agreed maturity of up to two years plus deposits redeemable at up to three months' notice.
- In America M3 consists of M2 plus institutional money funds, large time deposits, repurchase agreements and Eurodollars.
- In the Eurozone M3 equals M2 plus repurchase agreements, money-market funds and paper, and debt securities of up to two years' maturity.
- In Japan, the measure of broad money is M2 plus certificates of deposit. M2 consists of currency in circulation plus public- and private-sector deposits.

In Britain, there is no M3. The broad money measure is called M4. It consists of M0 plus sterling deposits held at British banks by the non-bank private sector.

Velocity of circulation

Velocity of circulation, that is, the number of times money changes hands in a year, may be measured by nominal GDP divided by any monetary aggregate such as M2 averaged over the year.

Monetary control

Monetary authorities attempt to control the size and growth of money in several ways.

- **Changing reserve-asset ratios.** This affects the multiple which banks can lend and is usually done only once every few years.
- **Open-market operations.** Buying or selling government bonds in the open market, which increases or reduces the amount of money in bank reserves and private deposits.
- **Influencing interest rates.** For example, by means of open-market operations (which affects the supply and demand for money), changing the discount rate, or imposing fixed rates for certain deposits or loans.
- **Credit controls.** For example, limits on total bank lending, total personal credit, or the margins that borrowers have to put up for any credit purchase.
- **Moral suasion.** For example, central banks hold heart-to-heart talks with commercial bankers, perhaps to persuade them to restrict lending.

Note that direct control over reserve-asset ratios and the monetary base affects the supply of money while the other measures affect demand for it.

Alternative indicators of monetary growth

Monetary growth can be tracked by watching the deposits which are included in the various monetary aggregates. Alternative approaches are to track the following.

- **The banking sector's balance sheet.** Movements on the liabilities side (deposits) must be matched by movements in assets (mainly loans) and liabilities not included in monetary aggregates.
- **Sectoral counterparts.** These are measured by money the public sector takes out of circulation (roughly, the budget surplus plus government bond sales to non-banks) plus net additions by the banking sector (mainly bank lending) plus net additions from overseas (net balance of payments inflows to the private sector).

Monetary targets

Monetary authorities adopt many approaches to monetary control. During the 1980s and for much of the 1990s, many central banks (in Britain, the Treasury) had explicit targets for chosen monetary aggregates.

This has largely fallen out of favour. Several central banks, including the European Central Bank, the Bank of England and the Central Bank of New Zealand, now have targets for inflation instead. Monetary growth is one of several indicators of economic activity that central bankers watch.

Although the European Central Bank targets inflation rather than monetary growth, it has a "reference value", reiterated in December 1999, of 4.5% for the annual rate of growth of M3. It thinks that this is the rate consistent with its inflation target (that consumer prices should rise by less than 2% per year), a trend rate of GDP growth of 2–2.5%, and an annual decline of 0.5–1% in the velocity of circulation of M3.

An important reason for the decline in the importance of monetary targets is Goodhart's law, which says that any monetary variable loses its usefulness within six months of being adopted as a target of monetary policy.

Even though monetary targets no longer enjoy the primacy they once did, central bankers and economists still watch monetary aggregates closely. In general, if a monetary aggregate is growing too rapidly, this may be an argument for the central bank to raise interest rates. Slow monetary growth is a sign of weakening economic activity, and may be an argument for lower rates. However, other signals of inflationary pressures will also be taken into account.

Money supply
Annual average % change

| | Narrow money | | | | Broad money | | | |
	1995	1996	1997	1998	1995	1996	1997	1998
Australia	6.5	14.0	13.3	5.9	8.5	10.6	7.3	9.4
Austria	14.8	4.7	4.7	...	5.0	2.6	2.1	...
Belgium	4.9	4.2	3.1	...	4.9	6.3	7.1	...
Canada	10.2	13.6	9.6	6.0	6.2	5.0	8.6	0.6
Denmark	4.6	11.5	5.7	4.8	6.2	8.1	6.8	1.7
France	1.4	5.4	4.1	8.6	10.8	4.0	7.3	11.0
Germany	7.0	12.2	2.0	10.0	4.6	7.5	2.2	4.4
Italy	0.4	4.9	6.5	11.1	2.3	2.2	-5.8	4.8
Japan	13.1	9.7	8.6	4.6	2.8	2.3	3.1	-1.6
Netherlands	13.5	12.1	7.8	...	5.9	5.6	6.8	...
Spain	2.9	7.1	14.0	15.8	6.6	2.9	1.5	2.0
Sweden	...	...	...	...	2.6	8.3	0.5	2.1
Switzerland	6.1	27.4	9.0	6.8	4.6	9.6	6.6	4.5
UK	16.7	9.3	25.7	9.8	13.2	10.7	3.7	8.3
US	-0.9	1.4	3.5	3.5	5.7	6.1	6.6	11.0

Sources: IMF.

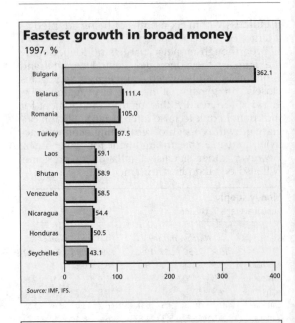

Fastest growth in broad money
1997, %

Bulgaria	362.1
Belarus	111.4
Romania	105.0
Turkey	97.5
Laos	59.1
Bhutan	58.9
Venezuela	58.5
Nicaragua	54.4
Honduras	50.5
Seychelles	43.1

Source: IMF, IFS.

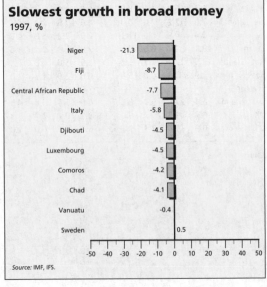

Slowest growth in broad money
1997, %

Niger	-21.3
Fiji	-8.7
Central African Republic	-7.7
Italy	-5.8
Djibouti	-4.5
Luxembourg	-4.5
Comoros	-4.2
Chad	-4.1
Vanuatu	-0.4
Sweden	0.5

Source: IMF, IFS.

Reserves

Official foreign reserves are roughly equivalent to a nation's bank balance. They consist of gold holdings, foreign currencies, special drawing rights (SDRs) and the country's reserve position in the International Monetary Fund.

Gold holdings have generally remained unchanged for years though the market value will vary with the price of gold. The world's developed economies own most of the world's gold, with the United States alone holding just over one-quarter of the world's total.

Reserves can be used to pay for imports, lessen the impact of economic shocks, service a country's debt, and defend its exchange rate. Strictly speaking, the level of reserves alone is not a guide to a country's ability to pay its way. That is determined in the short term at least by the government's ability to borrow overseas.

Gold reserves
End-1999

	Tonnes	% of total
IMF + BIS	3,420	10.2
Eurosystem	12,565	37.6
of which		
ECB	747	2.2
Germany	3,469	10.4
France	3,024	9.0
Italy	2,452	7.3
Other	2,874	8.6
US	8,137	24.3
Switzerland	2,590	7.8
Other developed countries	1,915	5.7
Developing countries	4,784	14.3
Total	33,412	100.0

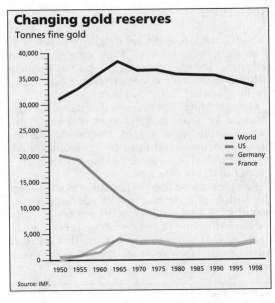

Changing gold reserves
Tonnes fine gold

- World
- US
- Germany
- France

Source: IMF.

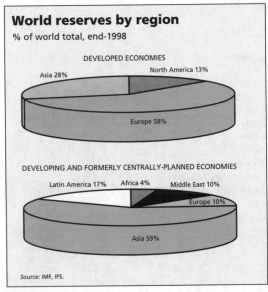

World reserves by region
% of world total, end-1998

DEVELOPED ECONOMIES

Asia 28%

North America 13%

Europe 58%

DEVELOPING AND FORMERLY CENTRALLY-PLANNED ECONOMIES

Latin America 17%   Africa 4%   Middle East 10%

Europe 10%

Asia 59%

Source: IMF, IFS.

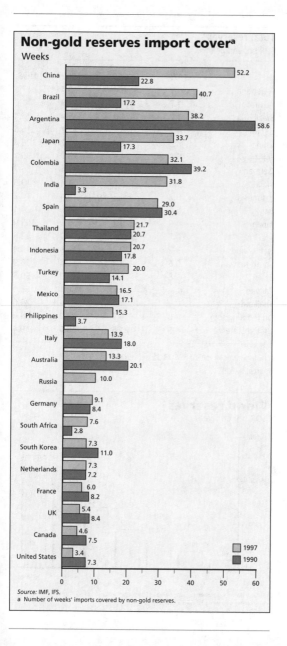

Non-gold reserves import cover[a]

Weeks

Country	1997	1990
China	52.2	22.8
Brazil	40.7	17.2
Argentina	38.2	58.6
Japan	33.7	17.3
Colombia	32.1	39.2
India	31.8	3.3
Spain	29.0	30.4
Thailand	21.7	20.7
Indonesia	20.7	17.8
Turkey	20.0	14.1
Mexico	16.5	17.1
Philippines	15.3	3.7
Italy	13.9	18.0
Australia	13.3	20.1
Russia	10.0	
Germany	9.1	8.4
South Africa	7.6	2.8
South Korea	7.3	11.0
Netherlands	7.3	7.2
France	6.0	8.2
UK	5.4	8.4
Canada	4.6	7.5
United States	3.4	7.3

Source: IMF, IFS.
a Number of weeks' imports covered by non-gold reserves.

Total reserves[a]
SDR bn, end-year

	1970	1980	1990	1998
Argentina	0.7	5.4	3.4	17.6
Australia	1.7	1.6	11.7	11.0
Brazil	1.2	4.6	5.4	30.4
Canada	4.7	3.2	13.1	16.6
China	n.a	2.4	21.2	106.4
France	5.0	24.3	28.7	35.1
Germany	13.6	41.4	51.1	56.7
India	1.0	5.7	1.4	19.8
Indonesia	0.2	4.3	5.4	16.2
Italy	5.4	20.5	46.6	24.1
Japan	4.8	20.2	56.0	153.9
Mexico	0.7	2.4	7.0	22.6
Netherlands	3.2	10.7	13.8	13.3
South Korea	0.6	2.3	10.4	36.9
Spain	1.8	9.8	12.9	50.3
Taiwan	n.a.	n.a.	58.1	63.0
Thailand	0.9	1.3	9.4	20.6
United Kingdom	2.8	16.9	25.9	24.0
United States	14.5	21.5	60.0	59.4

a Including gold valued at SDR 35 per ounce.
Source: IMF, IFS.

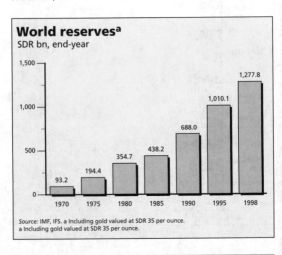

World reserves[a]
SDR bn, end-year

Year	Value
1970	93.2
1975	194.4
1980	354.7
1985	438.2
1990	688.0
1995	1,010.1
1998	1,277.8

Source: IMF, IFS. a Including gold valued at SDR 35 per ounce.
a Including gold valued at SDR 35 per ounce.

Notes and coins in circulation

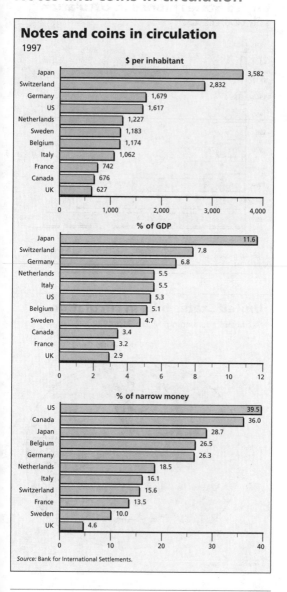

Notes and coins in circulation
1997

$ per inhabitant

Japan	3,582
Switzerland	2,832
Germany	1,679
US	1,617
Netherlands	1,227
Sweden	1,183
Belgium	1,174
Italy	1,062
France	742
Canada	676
UK	627

% of GDP

Japan	11.6
Switzerland	7.8
Germany	6.8
Netherlands	5.5
Italy	5.5
US	5.3
Belgium	5.1
Sweden	4.7
Canada	3.4
France	3.2
UK	2.9

% of narrow money

US	39.5
Canada	36.0
Japan	28.7
Belgium	26.5
Germany	26.3
Netherlands	18.5
Italy	16.1
Switzerland	15.6
France	13.5
Sweden	10.0
UK	4.6

Source: Bank for International Settlements.

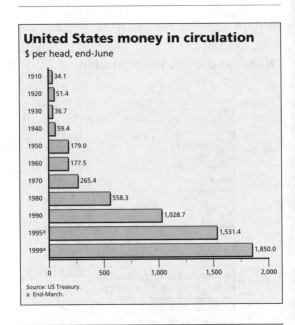

United States money in circulation

$ per head, end-June

Year	Value
1910	34.1
1920	51.4
1930	36.7
1940	59.4
1950	179.0
1960	177.5
1970	265.4
1980	558.3
1990	1,028.7
1995[a]	1,531.4
1999[a]	1,850.0

Source: US Treasury.
a End-March.

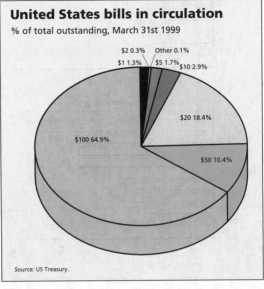

United States bills in circulation

% of total outstanding, March 31st 1999

$2 0.3%   Other 0.1%
$1 1.3% $5 1.7% $10 2.9%
$20 18.4%
$100 64.9%
$50 10.4%

Source: US Treasury.

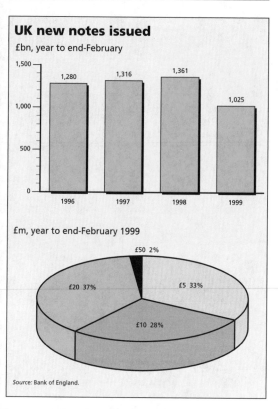

UK new notes issued

£bn, year to end-February

Year	Value
1996	1,280
1997	1,316
1998	1,361
1999	1,025

£m, year to end-February 1999

£50 2%
£5 33%
£10 28%
£20 37%

Source: Bank of England.

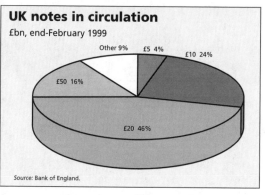

UK notes in circulation

£bn, end-February 1999

Other 9%
£5 4%
£10 24%
£50 16%
£20 46%

Source: Bank of England.

PART 4

THE VALUE
OF MONEY

Inflation

An increase in the general level of prices is nothing new: records from the days of the Roman Empire show rapid inflation. Since 1946 Britain's consumer prices have risen every year, but in fact inflation – in the sense of continuously rising prices – is historically the exception not the rule. Linking together various price series (of admittedly varying quality) suggests that in 1914, on the eve of the first world war, British consumer prices were no higher than during the 1660s. During those 250 years periods of rising prices were interspersed with periods of falling prices.

Inflation has three main adverse effects. First, it makes it hard to distinguish between changes in relative prices and changes in the general price level. This distorts the behaviour of individuals and firms, and so reduces economic efficiency. Second, its unpredictability creates uncertainty, which discourages investment. Third, inflation redistributes income: from creditors to borrowers; from those on fixed incomes to wage-earners.

It has become economic orthodoxy that price stability should be the goal of central banks. Many central banks now say that this is their aim, and several now have explicit inflation targets as the lodestar of monetary policy. For example the Bank of England is expected to achieve an inflation rate of 2.5% (excluding mortgage-interest payments). The European Central Bank's target is a rate of between zero and 2%. The Reserve Bank of New Zealand, a pioneer in inflation targeting, is supposed to keep inflation between zero and 3%.

Causes of inflation

There are two main theories about the causes of inflation; supply-shock and demand-pull. The reality is probably a complex mixture of the two.

Supply-shock (or cost-push). Prices are pushed up by higher wage and raw materials costs; perhaps owing to trade union power, dearer imports as a result of a weak currency, or a jump in commodity prices.

Demand-pull. Prices are pulled up when spending power (demand) is greater than the availability of goods and services. Factors which can boost aggregate demand include tax cuts, higher government spending, wage rises caused by labour shortages and an increase in consumer borrowing.

Recent experiences

Experiences with inflation range from deflation (a fall in prices experienced, for example, during the 1930s depression and by some oil-producing countries in the mid-1980s) to hyperinflation (such as when German wholesale prices rose by about 1.5 trillion % between 1919 and 1923). The most prominent recent example of deflation is Japan, where the consumer price index fell in the late 1990s. Hyperinflation is frequently associated with rapid increases in the money supply.

Industrial countries. Inflation was moderate in the industrial world in the 1960s, averaging about 3% a year. It jumped sharply after the two oil price shocks in the 1970s before falling again in the 1980s. In the fight to tame inflation, wage and price controls have generally given way to tight monetary and fiscal policies. Inflation has generally stayed low in industrial countries during the 1990s, thanks to a combination of weak commodity prices and cautious monetary policies.

Developing countries. Inflation generally accelerated in the developing countries in the 1980s, reaching over 1,000% in some Latin American countries. The early 1990s saw inflation surge in eastern Europe and the former Soviet Union as ex-communist countries struggled to adjust to a more market economy.

Since the mid 1990s inflation has moderated in

developing countries, falling from 51.8% in 1994 to 10.4% in 1998. Inflation slowed especially dramatically in Latin America – in Brazil, it dropped from over 2,000% in 1993 and 1994 to 3.5% in 1998 – and in central and eastern Europe and the former Soviet Union.

Inflation in the ancient world

There was only the most basic understanding of inflation in the ancient Greek and Roman world. Debasement (reducing the precious metal content) of the coinage was deprecated not because of its inflationary effects, but because it was regarded as immoral, on the grounds that the issuing authority was attempting to deceive consumers into thinking that they were getting something in their coinage that they were not.

Nevertheless, debasement was often resorted to by coin-issuing authorities, particularly by the Roman emperors. The Roman silver coinage (the denarius) was made of almost pure silver in the Republican period (c. 212–31BC), but by the reign of the emperor Nero (54–68AD) its silver content had dropped to 93%. By the end of the 2nd century AD the denarius contained only 50% silver, yet the coins circulated on a par with earlier, purer examples. By 270 the Roman coinage had declined to the level of a base-metal currency, with coins containing about 0.5% silver. The old, stable denominational structure had collapsed, but there were millions more coins in circulation and coinage was being far more widely used than it ever had been before. Just as inflation drove the farthing and the halfpenny out of circulation in the UK, so in the 3rd century low-denomination coins ceased to be made in Rome. The few figures that exist from the ancient world suggest that the 3rd and 4th centuries were a period of constant price inflation, either causing or fuelled by increased coin production. Lack of statistics preclude an estimation of the rate of inflation, but contemporary evidence from papyri in Egypt suggests a massive rise in prices of certain commodities, such as wheat, of the order of 1,000%, between AD246 and 294. Even the gold coinage, which until then had remained pure and stable, was debased and its weight fluctuated.

In 301 the reforming emperor Diocletian issued an edict fixing the prices of almost every sort of commodity, with the intention of protecting them from inflation and preventing social distress and unrest. The edict declares "Who does not know that wherever the common safety requires our armies to be sent, the profiteers insolently and covertly attack the public welfare? ... They charge extortionate prices for merchandise, not just four-fold or eightfold but on such a scale that human speech cannot find words to characterise their profit and their practices ... Aroused justly and rightfully by all the facts set forth above ... we have decided that maximum prices of articles for sale must be established." Examples are as follows:

1 army bushel of wheat	100 denarii
1 Italian pound (about 325g) of beef	8 denarii
1 Roman pound of gold	72,000 denarii
1 Roman pound of silver	6,000 denarii
1 day's wages for a farm labourer	25 denarii
A scribe, for writing 20 lines	20 denarii

The edict was ineffectual. People simply withdrew their goods from sale and no amount of official threats could control the constant increase in prices and the devaluation of the base-metal coinage, which continued throughout the 4th century. The gold coinage was returned to a stable standard, but the lower denominations were constantly declining and being reformed, more or less unsuccessfully.

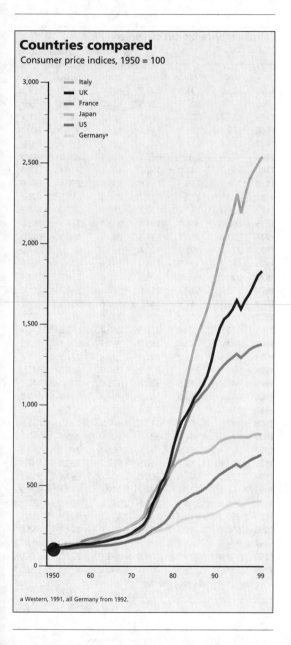

Countries compared

Consumer price indices, 1950 = 100

Italy
UK
France
Japan
US
Germany[a]

3,000

2,500

2,000

1,500

1,000

500

0

1950   60   70   80   90   99

a Western, 1991, all Germany from 1992.

Consumer price indices compared
1950 = 100

	UK	France	Germany[a]	Italy	Japan	US
1955	122.6	131.1	109.9	122.4	137.5	111.4
1960	137.6	172.3	120.5	134.2	148.4	123.2
1965	163.7	206.8	138.1	170.7	198.9	131.1
1966	170.1	212.1	143.1	174.8	208.7	135.2
1967	174.4	218.1	145.4	181.3	217.2	139.0
1968	182.5	228.1	147.7	183.8	229.0	144.8
1969	192.3	242.0	150.5	188.8	241.1	152.6
1970	204.7	256.3	155.6	198.0	259.4	161.6
1971	223.9	270.4	163.7	207.5	275.5	168.6
1972	239.7	287.2	172.7	219.4	287.9	174.2
1973	262.0	308.1	184.8	243.1	321.6	185.0
1974	303.8	350.3	197.7	289.5	400.1	205.3
1975	377.4	391.7	209.4	338.7	447.3	224.0
1976	440.2	429.3	218.4	395.6	488.9	237.0
1977	509.8	469.6	226.5	462.9	528.0	252.4
1978	552.1	512.4	232.6	518.9	548.1	271.6
1979	626.1	567.7	242.1	595.6	567.8	302.2
1980	738.5	643.2	255.2	721.9	613.2	343.0
1981	826.5	729.4	271.3	850.4	643.3	378.7
1982	897.4	815.4	285.7	990.7	660.0	402.2
1983	938.9	893.7	295.1	1,136.4	671.9	415.1
1984	985.9	959.9	302.2	1,259.1	687.3	432.9
1985	1,045.7	1,015.5	308.8	1,375.0	701.1	448.5
1986	1,081.6	1,040.9	308.5	1,456.1	705.3	457.0
1987	1,126.9	1,075.3	309.1	1,524.5	705.3	473.9
1988	1,182.1	1,104.3	313.1	1,600.7	710.2	492.9
1989	1,274.4	1,143.0	321.9	1,700.0	726.6	516.6
1990	1,395.3	1,181.8	330.6	1,807.1	749.1	544.5
1991	1,477.8	1,219.6	342.5	1,922.7	773.8	567.3
1992	1,532.5	1,248.9	360.0	2,024.6	787.0	584.3
1993	1,556.8	1,275.1	376.2	2,109.7	797.2	601.9
1994	1,595.9	1,296.4	380.9	2,192.8	803.2	617.1
1995	1,650.3	1,318.8	388.1	2,310.2	802.4	634.6
1996	1,690.0	1,345.2	393.5	2,402.6	803.3	653.0
1997	1,744.6	1,361.0	400.9	2,451.1	816.9	668.2
1998	1,803.8	1,371.6	404.8	2,499.6	822.5	679.0
1999	1,831.9	1,379.5	407.1	2,541.2	820.1	693.6

a Western, 1991, all Germany from 1992.

Consumer price changes compared
% change on a year earlier

	UK	France	Germany[a]	Italy	Japan	US
1965	4.6	2.7	3.2	4.5	6.7	1.6
1966	3.9	2.6	3.6	2.4	4.9	3.1
1967	2.5	2.8	1.6	3.7	4.1	2.8
1968	4.7	4.6	1.6	1.4	5.4	4.2
1969	5.4	6.1	1.9	2.7	5.3	5.4
1970	6.4	5.9	3.4	4.9	7.6	5.9
1971	9.4	5.5	5.2	4.8	6.2	4.3
1972	7.1	6.2	5.5	5.7	4.5	3.3
1973	9.3	7.3	7.0	10.8	11.7	6.2
1974	16.0	13.7	7.0	19.1	24.4	11.0
1975	24.2	11.8	5.9	17.0	11.8	9.1
1976	16.7	9.6	4.3	16.8	9.3	5.8
1977	15.8	9.4	3.7	17.0	8.0	6.5
1978	8.3	9.1	2.7	12.1	3.8	7.6
1979	13.4	10.8	4.1	14.8	3.6	11.3
1980	18.0	13.3	5.4	21.2	8.0	13.5
1981	11.9	13.4	6.3	17.8	4.9	10.4
1982	8.6	11.8	5.3	16.5	2.6	6.2
1983	4.6	9.6	3.3	14.7	1.8	3.2
1984	5.0	7.4	2.4	10.8	2.3	4.3
1985	6.1	5.8	2.2	9.2	2.0	3.6
1986	3.4	2.5	-0.1	5.9	0.6	1.9
1987	4.2	3.3	0.2	4.7	0.0	3.7
1988	4.9	2.7	1.3	5.0	0.7	4.0
1989	7.8	3.5	2.8	6.2	2.3	4.8
1990	9.5	3.4	2.7	6.3	3.1	5.4
1991	5.9	3.2	3.6	6.4	3.3	4.2
1992	3.7	2.4	5.1	5.3	1.7	3.1
1993	1.6	2.1	4.5	4.2	1.3	3.0
1994	2.5	1.7	2.7	3.9	0.8	2.5
1995	3.4	1.7	1.9	5.4	-0.1	2.8
1996	2.4	2.0	1.4	4.0	0.1	2.9
1997	3.2	1.2	1.9	2.0	1.7	2.3
1998	3.4	0.8	1.0	2.0	0.7	1.6
1999	1.6	0.6	0.6	1.7	-0.3	2.1

a Western, 1991, all Germany from 1992.

The pound in your pocket
Internal purchasing power of the pound

	1900	1910	1915	1920	1925
1900	100.0	106.3	146.8	341.8	184.8
1905	105.3	112.0	154.7	360.0	194.7
1910	94.0	100.0	138.1	321.4	173.8
1915	68.1	72.4	100.0	232.8	125.9
1920	29.3	31.1	43.0	100.0	54.1
1925	54.1	57.5	79.5	184.9	100.0
1930	76.0	80.8	111.5	259.6	140.4
1935	76.7	81.6	112.6	262.1	141.7
1940	52.0	55.3	76.3	177.6	96.1
1945	41.4	44.0	60.7	141.4	76.4
1950	33.8	35.9	49.6	115.4	62.4
1955	27.5	29.3	40.4	94.1	50.9
1960	24.5	26.1	36.0	83.9	45.3
1965	20.6	21.9	30.3	70.5	38.1
1970	16.5	17.5	24.2	56.4	30.5
1975	8.9	9.5	13.1	30.6	16.5
1980	4.6	4.9	6.7	15.6	8.4
1985	3.2	3.4	4.7	11.0	6.0
1990	2.4	2.6	3.6	8.3	4.5
1995	2.1	2.2	3.0	7.0	3.8
1999	1.9	2.0	2.7	6.3	3.4

	1960	1965	1970	1975	1980
1900	407.6	484.8	606.3	1,117.7	2,187.3
1905	429.3	510.7	638.7	1,177.3	2,304.0
1910	383.3	456.0	570.2	1,051.2	2,057.1
1915	277.6	330.2	412.9	761.2	1,489.7
1920	119.3	141.9	177.4	327.0	640.0
1925	220.5	262.3	328.1	604.8	1,183.6
1930	309.6	368.3	460.6	849.0	1,661.5
1935	312.6	371.8	465.0	857.3	1,677.7
1940	211.8	252.0	315.1	580.9	1,136.8
1945	168.6	200.5	250.8	462.3	904.7
1950	137.6	163.7	204.7	377.4	738.5
1955	112.2	133.4	166.9	307.7	602.1
1960	100.0	118.9	148.8	274.2	536.6
1965	84.1	100.0	125.1	230.5	451.2
1970	67.2	80.0	100.0	184.3	360.8
1975	36.5	43.4	54.2	100.0	195.7
1980	18.6	22.2	27.7	51.1	100.0
1985	13.2	15.7	19.6	36.1	70.6
1990	9.9	11.7	14.7	27.0	52.9
1995	8.4	9.9	12.4	22.9	44.8
1999	7.6	8.9	11.2	20.6	40.4

1930	1935	1940	1945	1950	1955
131.6	130.4	192.4	241.8	296.2	363.3
138.7	137.3	202.7	254.7	312.0	382.7
123.8	122.6	181.0	227.4	278.6	341.7
89.7	88.8	131.0	164.7	201.7	247.4
38.5	38.1	56.3	70.7	86.7	106.3
71.2	70.5	104.1	130.8	160.3	196.6
100.0	99.0	146.2	183.7	225.0	276.0
101.0	100.0	147.6	185.4	227.2	278.6
68.4	67.8	100.0	125.7	153.9	188.8
54.5	53.9	79.6	100.0	122.5	150.3
44.4	44.0	65.0	81.6	100.0	122.6
36.2	35.9	53.0	66.6	81.5	100.0
32.3	32.0	47.2	59.3	72.7	89.1
27.2	26.9	39.7	49.9	61.1	74.9
21.7	21.5	31.7	39.9	48.9	59.9
11.8	11.7	17.2	21.6	26.5	32.5
6.0	6.0	8.8	11.1	13.5	16.6
4.3	4.2	6.2	7.8	9.6	11.7
3.2	3.2	4.7	5.8	7.2	8.8
2.7	2.7	3.9	5.0	5.1	7.4
2.4	2.4	3.5	4.5	4.6	6.7

1985	1990	1995	1999
3,097.5	4,132.9	4,878.9	5,412.3
3,262.7	4,353.3	5,139.0	5,700.8
2,913.1	3,886.9	4,588.5	5,090.1
2,109.5	2,814.7	3,322.7	3,685.9
906.3	1,209.3	1,427.6	1,583.7
1,676.0	2,236.3	2,639.9	2,928.5
2,352.9	3,139.4	3,706.1	4,111.3
2,375.7	3,169.9	3,742.1	4,151.2
1,609.9	2,148.0	2,535.7	2,812.9
1,281.2	1,709.4	2,018.0	2,238.6
1,045.7	1,395.3	1,647.2	1,827.3
852.6	1,137.6	1,342.9	1,489.7
759.9	1,014.0	1,197.0	1,327.9
638.9	852.5	1,006.4	1,116.4
510.9	681.6	804.7	892.7
277.1	369.8	436.5	484.2
141.6	188.9	223.0	247.4
100.0	133.4	157.5	174.7
74.9	100.0	118.1	131.0
63.5	84.7	100.0	110.9
57.2	76.4	90.1	100.0

For help with using the table, note that:
• in 1999 the pound was worth 1.9p compared with its value in 1900 and 7.6p compared with its value in 1960
• compared with its value in 1999, the pound was worth 54.1 times more in 1900 and 13.2 times more in 1960.

The dollar in your pocket
Internal purchasing power of the dollar

	1913	1915	1920	1925	1930
1913	100	102	202	177	169
1915	98	100	198	173	165
1920	50	51	100	88	84
1925	57	58	114	100	95
1930	59	60	120	105	100
1935	72	74	146	128	122
1940	71	72	143	125	119
1945	55	56	111	97	93
1950	41	42	83	73	69
1955	37	38	75	65	62
1960	33	34	68	59	56
1965	31	32	63	56	53
1970	26	26	52	45	43
1975	18	19	37	33	31
1980	12	12	24	21	20
1985	9	9	19	16	16
1990	8	8	15	13	13
1995	6	7	13	11	11
1999	6	6	12	11	10

	1960	1965	1970	1975	1980
1913	299	318	390	1320	832
1915	293	312	382	533	816
1920	148	158	193	269	412
1925	169	180	221	307	471
1930	177	189	231	322	493
1935	216	230	282	393	601
1940	211	225	276	384	589
1945	164	175	214	299	458
1950	123	131	160	223	342
1955	110	118	144	201	307
1960	100	106	130	182	278
1965	94	100	123	171	262
1970	77	82	100	139	213
1975	55	59	72	100	153
1980	36	38	47	65	100
1985	28	29	36	50	77
1990	23	24	30	41	63
1995	19	21	25	35	54
1999	18	19	23	32	49

1935	1940	1945	1950	1955
138	141	182	243	271
136	139	178	239	265
69	70	90	121	134
78	80	103	138	153
82	84	108	144	160
100	102	131	176	196
98	100	129	172	191
76	78	100	134	149
57	58	75	100	111
51	52	67	90	100
46	47	61	81	91
43	44	57	77	85
35	36	47	62	69
25	26	33	45	50
17	17	22	29	33
13	13	17	22	25
10	11	14	18	21
9	9	12	16	18
8	8	11	14	16

1985	1990	1995	1999
1,087	1,320	1,539	1,683
1,065	1,294	1,509	1,650
538	654	762	833
615	747	871	952
644	783	913	998
785	954	1112	1216
769	934	1089	1190
598	726	847	926
446	542	632	691
401	488	569	622
364	442	515	563
342	415	484	529
279	339	395	432
200	243	283	310
131	159	185	202
100	121	142	155
82	100	117	127
71	86	100	109
65	78	91	100

For help with using the table, note that:
• in 1999 the dollar was worth 6 cents compared with its value in 1913 and 18 cents compared with its value in 1960
• compared with its value in 1999, the dollar was worth 16.8 times more in 1913 and 5.6 times more in 1960.

Highest inflation, 1998–99
% consumer price inflation

1	Belarus	293.7	21	Myanmar	18.4
2	Congo[a]	175.5	22	Sudan[b]	17.1
3	Laos	128.4	23	Mexico	16.6
4	Tajikistan[a]	87.8	24	Ukraine[a]	15.9
5	Russia	85.7	25	Papua New Guinea	14.9
6	Turkmenistan[a]	84.0	26	Ghana[b]	14.6
7	Angola[b]	74.7	27	Honduras	11.6
8	Uzbekistan[a]	72.0	28	Colombia	11.2
9	Turkey	64.9		Nicaragua	11.2
10	Ecuador	52.2	30	Slovakia	10.6
11	Moldova	45.9	31	Hungary	10.3
12	Romania	45.8	32	Costa Rica	10.0
13	Malawi	44.9	33	Madagascar	9.9
14	Kirgizstan	35.9	34	Lesotho[c]	9.3
15	Sierra Leone	34.1	35	Armenia[b]	8.7
16	Zimbabwe[b]	31.8		Haiti	8.7
17	Zambia[a]	24.8		Vietnam[b]	8.7
18	Venezuela	23.6	38	Bhutan[b]	8.5
19	Iran	21.0	39	Bangladesh[a]	8.3
20	Indonesia	20.5	40	Kazakhstan	8.2

Highest inflation, 1990–99
% consumer price inflation

1	Congo[d]	1,710.5	16	Macedonia[e]	116.3
2	Turkmenistan[d]	668.4	17	Romania	113.9
3	Tajikistan[d]	467.6	18	Croatia	105.9
4	Ukraine[d]	431.3	19	Lithuania	105.1
5	Armenia[e]	405.4	20	Sudan[e]	85.8
6	Georgia[e]	395.6	21	Suriname[d]	84.8
7	Belarus	353.4	22	Estonia	80.3
8	Azerbaijan[d]	333.6	23	Turkey	78.7
9	Uzbekistan[d]	296.4	24	Zambia[d]	77.9
10	Brazil	236.3	25	Latvia	73.0
11	Kazakhstan	231.5	26	Nicaragua	63.2
12	Russia	190.8	27	Mongolia[f]	59.3
13	Moldova	151.8	28	Venezuela	46.7
14	Kirgizstan	131.3	29	Peru	42.5
15	Bulgaria	123.5	30	Guinea-Bissau[e]	41.3

a 1996–97   b 1997–98   c 1995–96   d 1990–97   e 1990–98   f 1992–99

Lowest inflation, 1998–99
% consumer price inflation

1	Chad	-6.8		Taiwan	0.2
2	Bulgaria	-5.5	22	Benin	0.3
3	Hong Kong	-4.0		Thailand	0.3
4	Ethiopia[a]	-3.7	24	Albania	0.4
5	Rwanda	-2.4		Singapore	0.4
6	Niger	-2.3	26	El Salvador	0.5
7	Central African Rep[b]	-1.9		France	0.5
8	Saudi Arabia	-1.6		Macedonia[b]	0.5
9	China	-1.4		Sweden	0.5
10	Argentina	-1.2	30	Austria	0.6
	Mali	-1.2		Germany	0.6
	Syria[b]	-1.2	32	Morocco	0.7
13	Burkina Faso	-1.1	33	Côte d'Ivoire	0.8
14	Bahrain[b]	-0.4		Lithuania	0.8
15	Japan	-0.3		Senegal	0.8
16	Congo-Brazzaville[c]	-0.2		South Korea	0.8
17	New Zealand	-0.1		Switzerland	0.8
	Togo	-0.1	38	Luxembourg	1.0
19	Cameroon[b]	0.1	39	Belgium	1.1
20	Kuwait[b]	0.2		Netherlands Antilles[b]	1.1

Lowest inflation, 1990–99
% consumer price inflation

1	Bahrain[e]	1.0	16	Austria	2.3
	Japan	1.0		Kuwait [e]	2.3
3	Panama	1.2		Norway	2.3
	Saudi Arabia	1.2	19	Sweden	2.4
5	Finland	1.7	20	Germany	2.5
	France	1.7		Netherlands	2.5
	New Zealand	1.7		Netherlands Antilles[e]	2.5
8	Singapore	1.8	23	Bahamas	2.6
9	Canada	1.9	24	Taiwan	2.7
10	Australia	2.0		United States	2.7
	Belgium	2.0	26	Barbados	2.8
	Switzerland	2.0	27	Malta	2.9
13	Denmark	2.1	28	Iceland	3.0
	Luxembourg	2.1		Qatar[d]	3.0
15	Ireland	2.2	30	United Kingdom	3.1

Notes: Inflation is measured as the % increase in the consumer price index between two dates. The figures shown are based on the average level of the index during the relevant years.

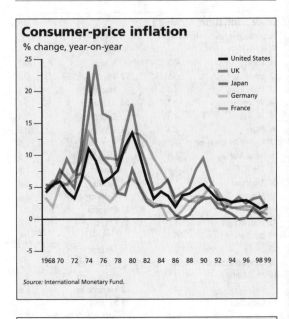

Consumer-price inflation

% change, year-on-year

United States
UK
Japan
Germany
France

1968 70 72 74 76 78 80 82 84 86 88 90 92 94 96 98 99

Source: International Monetary Fund.

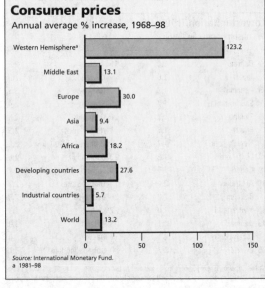

Consumer prices

Annual average % increase, 1968–98

Western Hemisphere[a]	123.2
Middle East	13.1
Europe	30.0
Asia	9.4
Africa	18.2
Developing countries	27.6
Industrial countries	5.7
World	13.2

0   50   100   150

Source: International Monetary Fund.
a 1981–98

Exchange rates

Exchange rates are nothing more than the price of one currency in terms of another. They are determined mainly by supply and demand, which reflect trade and other international payments, and, much more important, volatile capital flows which are constantly shifting around the world in search of the best expected investment returns.

A history of exchange rates

The easiest way to understand exchange rates and their influence on the balance of payments is to review previous experiences.

The gold standard. Before 1914 exchange rates were fixed in terms of gold, trade was mainly in physical goods and capital flows were limited. A country which developed a deficit on its current account would first consume its reserves of foreign currencies. Then it would have to pay for the imports by shipping gold. The transfer of gold would reduce the money supply in the deficit country and boost it elsewhere, since currencies were then backed by convertibility into gold.

In the deficit country the contracting money supply would tend to depress output and prices. Elsewhere the expanding money supply would boost output and inflation. The deficit country could then only afford to import a lower quantity of dearer foreign goods. The surplus countries could import a higher quantity of the deficit country's cheaper goods. Thus the current account would automatically return to equilibrium.

That was the theory. It seemed to work in practice until the system got out of balance in the 1920s. The gold standard was temporarily suspended during the first world war. Countries experienced rapid and varying rates of inflation and exports were grossly underpriced or overpriced when the gold standard was reintroduced at pre-war rates. Large current-account surpluses and deficits developed. The gold standard fell from favour and was abandoned almost universally by the early 1930s.

The 1930s. There were widespread experiments with fixed and floating exchange rates during the 1930s. Almost every country tried to alleviate the unemployment of the Depression by limiting imports and boosting exports with measures such as import duties, quotas and exchange-rate devaluation or depreciation. It may seem obvious, but world exports cannot rise if world imports fall. The international payments system fell further into disrepute.

Adjustable pegs. An international conference was convened in America at Bretton Woods, New Hampshire, in June 1944. Participants agreed to form the IMF and World Bank to promote international monetary cooperation and the major currencies were fixed in relation to the dollar. Fluctuations were limited to 1% in either direction, although larger revaluations and devaluations were allowed with IMF permission. In addition, the American government agreed to buy gold on demand at just over $35 an ounce, which left only the dollar on a gold standard.

Floating rates. The Bretton Woods system broke down by the 1970s. Persistent American deficits had led to an international excess of dollars and American gold reserves came under pressure. In August 1971 the Americans suspended the convertibility of the dollar, imposed a 10% surcharge on imports and took other measures aimed at eliminating its balance of payments deficit. The major currencies were allowed to float, some within constraints imposed by exchange controls (dirty floats).

Fixed rates with some flexibility were reintroduced in December 1971 following a meeting of the IMF Group of Ten at the Smithsonian Institute in Washington (the "Smithsonian agreement"). However, sterling was floated "temporarily" in

June 1972 and by the following year all major currencies were floating or subject to managed floats. Despite bouts of extreme turbulence, most major currencies have remained floating ever since. The exceptions are EU currencies. Several of these spent the 1980s and most of the 1990s linked to one another in the exchange-rate mechanism of the European monetary system. At the start of 1999, eleven countries fixed their exchange rates irrevocably by joining a single European currency, the euro. The euro floats freely against other currencies.

What determines exchange rates

There is no neat explanation for what determines exchange rates. The two main theories are based on purchasing power and asset markets (investment portfolios).

Purchasing power parity (PPP). The traditional approach to exchange rates says that they move to keep international purchasing power in line (parity). If American inflation is 6% and Canadian inflation is 4%, the American dollar will fall by 2% to maintain PPP. With floating exchange rates this would happen automatically. If exchange rates are fixed, demand pressures will instead equalise inflation in the two countries.

Another version of this, favoured by some economists, is to define purchasing power parity as the exchange rate which equates the prices of a basket of goods and services in two countries. In the long term, it is argued, currencies should move towards their PPP. *The Economist* has a simpler approach with its Big Mac index. The index offers a guide to whether currencies are at their "correct" level. It is based on "purchasing-power parity" – the notion that an identical basket of goods and services should cost the same in all countries. The Big Mac PPP is the exchange rate at which hamburgers would cost the same in America as abroad. The chart on the next page calculates the over- or undervaluation of emerging-market currencies against the dollar at the turn of the century. For

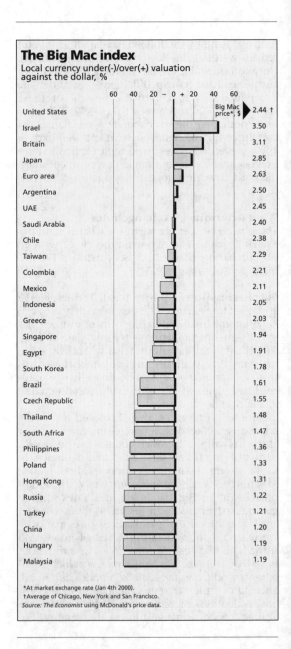

The Big Mac index

Local currency under(-)/over(+) valuation
against the dollar, %

Country	Big Mac price*, $
United States	2.44 †
Israel	3.50
Britain	3.11
Japan	2.85
Euro area	2.63
Argentina	2.50
UAE	2.45
Saudi Arabia	2.40
Chile	2.38
Taiwan	2.29
Colombia	2.21
Mexico	2.11
Indonesia	2.05
Greece	2.03
Singapore	1.94
Egypt	1.91
South Korea	1.78
Brazil	1.61
Czech Republic	1.55
Thailand	1.48
South Africa	1.47
Philippines	1.36
Poland	1.33
Hong Kong	1.31
Russia	1.22
Turkey	1.21
China	1.20
Hungary	1.19
Malaysia	1.19

*At market exchange rate (Jan 4th 2000).
†Average of Chicago, New York and San Francisco.
Source: The Economist using McDonald's price data.

example, dividing the local-currency price of a Big Mac in Brazil by its American price produced a dollar PPP of 1.2 *reais* when the actual dollar rate was 1.84 reais – therefore the currency was 34% undervalued.

Portfolio balance. The portfolio approach suggests that exchange rates move to balance total returns (interest plus expected exchange-rate movements). If yen deposits pay 6% and dollar deposits pay 8%, investors will buy dollars for the higher return until the exchange rate has been pushed up so far that the dollar is expected to depreciate by 2%. The expected return from the dollar will then exactly match the expected return from the yen.

Overshooting. The best guess is that exchange rates are determined by PPP in the long run, but that this is overridden in the short term by portfolio pressures. These tend to cause currencies to overshoot PPP equilibrium.

Who determines exchange rates

Clearly there is a complex interaction between exchange rates and various economic and financial variables, many of which are outside domestic control (they are determined exogenously). Central banks can either try to control these variables in order to fix their exchange rate, or leave the exchange rate to the markets.

In fact, of the 150 or so main currencies in 1990, less than one-fifth were freely floating, including those of Australia, Canada, Japan, Switzerland and America. Of the remaining currencies, 30 had managed floats or limited flexibility, while around 30 were pegged to the dollar, 14 to the French franc, five to other single currencies and 40 to the SDR or other baskets of currencies. By 2000, however, some 50 of the world's 180-odd currencies were freely floating.

Monetary policy. All economic policies affect exchange rates, although changes in interest rates have probably the most direct and visible influence. The exchange rate is thus the broadest indicator of monetary policy.

Intervention. Central banks frequently intervene in the currency markets. They buy or sell their currency in order to alter the balance of supply and demand and move the exchange rate. This is essentially a short-term smoothing activity since they can buy one currency only if they have another to sell.

Effects of exchange-rate movements
The most immediate effect of a weaker currency is higher domestic inflation owing to dearer imports. At the same time, exports priced in foreign currencies and inflows of rents, interest, profits and dividends generate more income in domestic-currency terms. Thus the trade and current-account balances deteriorate.

Later, after perhaps as much as 12–18 months, relative price movements cause a shift from imports to domestic production and exports. This boosts GDP and the trade and current accounts improve. (Their deterioration followed by improvement is known as the J-curve effect.) However, higher inflation caused by a weaker currency can wipe out any current account improvement within a number of years.

Capital account. With regard to the capital account of the balance of payments, a weaker currency makes inward investment look more attractive. In foreign-currency terms outlays are lower and returns are higher, but this may not be enough to attract investors if the currency weakened because of unfavourable domestic economic conditions.

Exchange rates
Currency rates per $, period average

Country	Currency	1980	1985	1990	1995	1999
Australia	dollar	0.88	1.43	1.28	1.35	1.60
Austria	schilling	12.94	20.69	11.37	10.08	12.38
Belgium	franc	29.25	59.43	33.42	29.50	36.30
Canada	dollar	1.17	1.37	1.17	1.37	1.48
Denmark	krone	5.64	10.59	6.19	5.60	6.70
France	franc	4.23	8.98	5.45	4.99	5.90
Germany	D-mark	1.82	2.94	1.62	1.43	1.76
Italy	lira	831.00	1,909.00	1,198.00	1,629.00	1,736.00
Japan	yen	226.70	238.60	144.80	94.10	130.90
Netherlands	guilder	1.99	3.32	1.82	1.61	1.99
Spain	peseta	71.70	170.10	101.90	124.70	149.40
Sweden	krona	4.23	8.60	5.92	7.13	7.95
Switzerland	franc	1.68	2.46	1.39	1.18	1.45
UK	pound	0.43	0.78	0.56	0.63	0.60
US	dollar	1.00	1.00	1.00	1.00	1.00
SDR		0.78	0.99	0.74	0.69	0.74
ECU		1.31	1.32	0.79	0.77	0.89

Source: IMF.

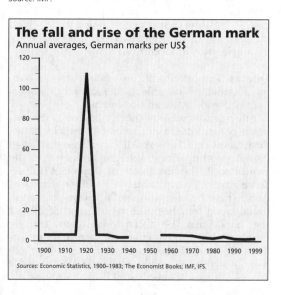

The fall and rise of the German mark
Annual averages, German marks per US$

Sources: Economic Statistics, 1900–1983; The Economist Books; IMF, IFS.

Special Drawing Rights (SDR)

The SDR (Special Drawing Right) has some of the characteristics of a world currency. It was introduced by the IMF in 1970 to boost world liquidity after the ratio of world reserves to imports had fallen by half since the 1950s.

Advantages. The SDR is stable. It is used for accounting purposes by the IMF and even some multinational corporations. Commercial banks accept deposits and make loans in SDRs, and it is used to price some international transactions.

Disadvantages. Since the SDR is an average of four currencies it is less valuable than the strongest and is among the first to go when reserves are sold off.

Value. SDRs were first allocated in 1970 equal to $1/35$ of an ounce of gold, or exactly $1 ($1.0857 after the dollar was devalued in 1971). When the dollar came off the gold standard the SDR was fixed from 1974 in terms of a basket of 16 currencies. In 1981 the basket was slimmed to five. With the creation of the euro in 1999, the number of currencies was reduced to four.

Quotas. The IMF allocates to each member country a quota which reflects the country's importance in world trade and payments.

Any member with balance of payments difficulties may swap its SDRs for reserve currencies at IMF-designated central banks. It can also use its own currency to buy (draw) foreign currency from the Fund's pool. The first chunk of currencies (the reserve tranche), amounting to 25% of the member's quota, may be taken unconditionally. Four additional credit tranches each worth another 25% of the quota may be taken under progressively tougher terms and conditions. When these options are used up there are other borrowing facilities available. The IMF also arranges standby credits in times of severe strain on a currency.

SDR exchange rates
Currency units per SDR, period average

Country	Currency	1980	1985	1990	1995	1998
Australia	dollar	1.52	1.54	1.65	2.05	2.29
Austria	schilling	17.61	18.98	15.19	15.29	16.54
Belgium	franc	40.21	55.32	44.08	44.75	48.68
Canada	dollar	1.52	1.54	1.65	2.08	2.16
Denmark	krone	7.67	9.85	8.22	8.50	8.99
France	franc	4.90	5.95	5.17	7.57	7.92
Germany	D-mark	2.50	2.70	2.13	2.17	2.36
Italy	lira	1,186.80	1,843.70	1,607.80	2,471.11	2,327.60
Japan	yen	258.91	220.23	191.21	142.75	162.77
Netherlands	guilder	2.72	3.05	2.40	2.44	2.66
Spain	peseta	101.08	169.32	137.87	189.16	200.79
Sweden	krona	5.58	8.37	8.11	10.82	11.35
Switzerland	franc	2.25	2.28	1.84	1.79	1.94
UK	pound	0.54	0.76	0.74	0.96	0.85
US	dollar	1.28	1.10	1.42	1.52	1.36

Source: IMF.

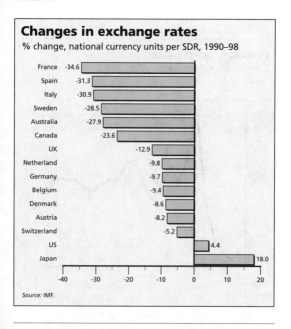

Changes in exchange rates
% change, national currency units per SDR, 1990–98

Country	% change
France	-34.6
Spain	-31.3
Italy	-30.9
Sweden	-28.5
Australia	-27.9
Canada	-23.6
UK	-12.9
Netherland	-9.8
Germany	-9.7
Belgium	-9.4
Denmark	-8.6
Austria	-8.2
Switzerland	-5.2
US	4.4
Japan	18.0

Source: IMF.

Gold and silver

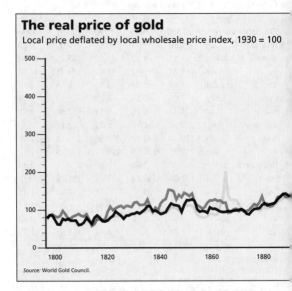

The real price of gold
Local price deflated by local wholesale price index, 1930 = 100

Source: World Gold Council.

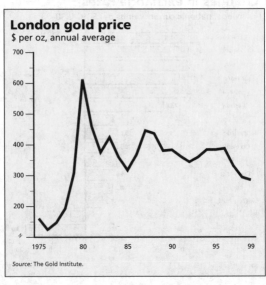

London gold price
$ per oz, annual average

Source: The Gold Institute.

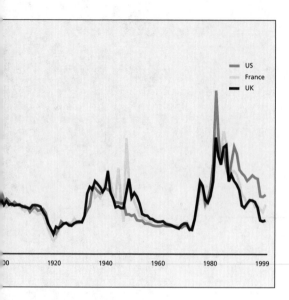

US
France
UK

00   1920   1940   1960   1980   1999

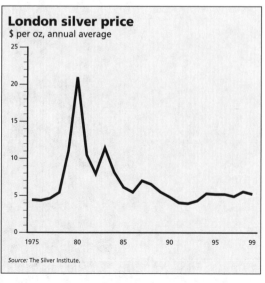

London silver price
$ per oz, annual average

25

20

15

10

5

0

1975   80   85   90   95   99

Source: The Silver Institute.

PART 5

THE BUSINESS
OF MONEY

Foreign exchange markets

The foreign-exchange markets underpin all other financial markets. They directly influence each country's foreign-trade patterns, determine the flow of international investment and affect domestic interest and inflation rates. They operate in every corner of the world, in every single currency. Collectively, they form the largest financial market by far. An estimated 150,000 foreign-exchange transactions occur every day, with an average turnover totalling $1.5 trillion a day.

Foreign-exchange trading dates back to ancient times, and has flourished or diminished depending on the extent of international commerce and the monetary arrangements of the day. In medieval times, coins minted from gold or silver circulated freely across the borders of Europe's duchies and kingdoms, and foreign-exchange traders provided one form of coinage in trade for another. By the late 14th century bankers in Italy were dealing in paper debits or credits issued in assorted currencies, discounted according to the bankers' judgment of the currencies' relative values. This allowed international trade to expand far more than would have been possible if trading partners had to rely on barter.

Yet foreign-exchange trading remained a minor part of finance. When paper money came into widespread use in the 18th century, its value too was determined mainly by the amount of silver or gold that the government promised to pay the bearer. As this amount changed infrequently, businesses and investors faced little risk that exchange-rate movements would greatly affect their profits. There was little need to trade foreign currencies except in connection with a specific transaction, such as an export sale or the purchase of a company abroad.

It is really only since the collapse of the Bretton Woods system (see page 82) and the resulting uncertainty about the level of exchange rates that foreign exchange trading has grown dramatically.

Geographic distribution of traditional currency trading[a]

| | April 1989 | | April 1998 | |
	Average daily turnover ($bn)	% share	Average daily turnover ($bn)	% share
UK	184.0	26	637.3	32
US	115.2	16	350.9	18
Japan	110.8	15	148.6	8
Singapore	55.0	8	139.0	7
Germany	n/a	n/a	94.3	5
Switzerland	56.0	8	81.7	4
Hong Kong	48.8	7	78.6	4
France	23.2	3	71.9	4
Australia	28.9	4	46.6	2
Netherlands	12.9	2	41.0	2

a Traditional products include spot transactions, forwards and foreign-exchange swaps.

Traditional foreign-exchange trading, by currency[a], April 1998

	% of average daily turnover[b]
US dollar	43.5
D-mark	15.0
Japanese yen	10.5
UK £	5.5
Swiss franc	3.5
French franc	2.5
Canadian $	2.0
Australian $	1.5
ECU & other EMS currencies[c]	8.5
Other currencies	7.5

a Traditional includes spot transactions, forwards and foreign-exchange swaps.
b Published figures double-count transactions; figures in this table represent half of official totals.
c The ECU is the European Currency Unit, former accounting currency of the EU. Other EMS currencies include Austrian schilling, Belgian franc, Danish krone, Finnish markka, Irish punt, Italian lira, Netherlands guilder, Portuguese escudo, Spanish peseta.
Source for both tables: Bank for International Settlements.

Largest exchange-rate futures contracts, 1998

Contract	Exchange	No.traded
US dollars	Bolsa de Mercadorias & Futuros, Brazil	18,573,100
Japanese yen	Chicago Mercantile Exchange	7,065,266
D-marks	Chicago Mercantile Exchange	6,884,026
Swiss francs	Chicago Mercantile Exchange	3,974,163
UK £	Chicago Mercantile Exchange	2,625,017
Canadian $	Chicago Mercantile Exchange	2,396,300
Mexican pesos	Chicago Mercantile Exchange	1,353,867

Source: Exchange reports.

Traditional foreign-exchange trading, by currency[a], April 1998

	% of average daily turnover[b]
US dollar	43.5
D-mark	15.0
Japanese yen	10.5
UK £	5.5
Swiss franc	3.5
French franc	2.5
Canadian $	2.0
Australian $	1.5
ECU & other EMS currencies[c]	8.5
Other currencies	7.5

a Traditional includes spot transactions, forwards and foreign-exchange swaps.
b Published figures double-count transactions; figures in this table represent half of official totals.
c The ECU is the European Currency Unit, former accounting currency of the EU. Other EMS currencies include Austrian schilling, Belgian franc, Danish krone, Finnish markka, Irish punt, Italian lira, Netherlands guilder, Portuguese escudo, Spanish peseta.
Source: Bank for International Settlements.

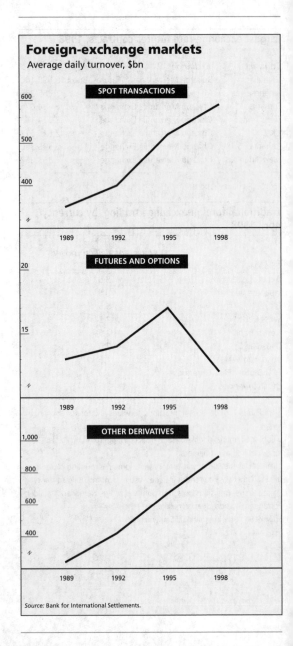

Foreign-exchange markets
Average daily turnover, $bn

SPOT TRANSACTIONS

600
500
400

1989   1992   1995   1998

FUTURES AND OPTIONS

20
15

1989   1992   1995   1998

OTHER DERIVATIVES

1,000
800
600
400

1989   1992   1995   1998

Source: Bank for International Settlements.

Money markets

The term "money market" refers to the network of corporations, financial institutions, investors and governments which deal with the flow of short-term capital. When a business needs cash for a couple of months, or when a bank wants to invest money that depositors may withdraw at any moment, or when a government tries to meet its payroll in the face of big seasonal fluctuations in tax receipts, the short-term liquidity transactions occur in the money market.

The money markets have expanded significantly in recent years as a result of the general outflow of money from the banking industry, a process referred to as disintermediation. Until the start of the 1980s, financial markets in almost all countries were centred on commercial banks. Savers and investors kept most of their assets on deposit with banks, either as short-term demand deposits, such as cheque-writing accounts, paying little or no interest, or in the form of certificates of deposit that tied up the money for years. Drawing on this reliable supply of low-cost money, banks were the main source of credit for businesses and consumers.

Financial deregulation has caused banks to lose market share in both deposit gathering and lending. This trend has been encouraged by legislation, such as the Monetary Control Act of 1980 in the United States, which allowed market forces rather than regulators to determine interest rates. Investors can place their money on deposit with investment companies that offer competitive interest rates without requiring a long-term commitment. Many borrowers can sell short-term debt to the same sorts of entities, also at competitive rates, rather than negotiating loans from bankers. The money markets are the mechanism that brings these borrowers and investors together without the comparatively costly intermediation of banks. They make it possible for borrowers to meet short-run liquidity needs and deal with irregular cash flows without resorting to more costly means of raising money.

There is an identifiable money market for each currency, because interest rates vary from one currency to another. These markets are not independent, and both investors and borrowers will shift from one currency to another depending upon relative interest rates. However, regulations limit the ability of some investors to hold foreign-currency instruments, and most money-market investors are concerned to minimise any risk of loss as a result of exchange-rate fluctuations. For these reasons, most money-market transactions occur in the investor's home currency.

The money markets do not exist in a particular place or operate according to a single set of rules. Nor do they offer a single set of posted prices, with one current interest rate for money. Rather, they are webs of borrowers and lenders, all linked by telephones and computers. At the centre of each web is the central bank whose policies determine the short-term interest rates for that currency. Arrayed around the central bankers are the treasurers of tens of thousands of businesses and government agencies, whose job is to invest any unneeded cash as safely and profitably as possible and, when necessary, to borrow at the lowest possible cost. The connections among them are established by banks and investment companies that trade securities as their main business. The constant soundings among these diverse players for the best available rate at a particular moment are the force that keeps the market competitive.

The Bank for International Settlements, which compiles statistics gathered by national central banks, estimates that the total amount of money-market instruments in circulation worldwide at March 1999 was $5.4 trillion, representing a gradual but steady increase compared with the $4 trillion outstanding at the end of 1995.

Types of instruments
There are numerous types of money-market instruments. The best known are commercial paper, bankers' acceptances, treasury bills, government

agency notes, local government notes, interbank loans, time deposits and paper issued by international organisations. The amount issued during the course of a year is much greater than the amount outstanding at any one time, as many money-market securities are outstanding for only short periods of time.

Commercial paper is a short-term debt obligation of a private-sector firm or a government-sponsored corporation. In most cases, the paper has a lifetime, or maturity, greater than 90 days but less than nine months.

Bankers' acceptances. An acceptance is a promissory note issued by a non-financial firm to a bank in return for a loan. The bank resells the note in the money market at a discount and guarantees payment. Acceptances usually have a maturity of less than six months.

Bankers' acceptances differ from commercial paper in significant ways. They are usually tied to the sale or storage of specific goods, such as an export order for which the proceeds will be received in two or three months. They are not issued at all by financial-industry firms. They do not bear interest; instead, an investor purchases the acceptance at a discount from face value and then redeems it for face value at maturity. Investors rely on the strength of the guarantor bank, rather than of the issuing company, for their security.

In an era when banks were able to borrow at lower cost than other types of firms, bankers' acceptances allowed manufacturers to take advantage of banks' superior credit standing. This advantage has largely disappeared, as many other big corporate borrowers are considered at least as creditworthy as banks.

Treasury bills, often referred to as T-bills, are securities with a maturity of one year or less, issued by national governments. Treasury bills issued by a government in its own currency are generally considered the safest of all possible investments in that currency. Such securities account for a larger share of money-market trading than any other type of instrument.

Government agency notes. National government agencies and government-sponsored corporations are heavy borrowers in the money markets in many countries. These include entities such as development banks, housing finance corporations, education lending agencies and agricultural finance agencies.

Local government notes are issued by state, provincial or local governments, and by agencies of these governments such as schools authorities and transport commissions. The ability of governments at this level to issue money-market securities varies greatly from country to country.

Interbank loans. Loans from one bank to another with which it has no affiliation are called interbank loans. Many of these loans are across international boundaries and are used by the borrowing institution to re-lend to its own customers. In December 1998 banks had a net $374 billion outstanding to banks in other countries, with almost all of this amount maturing with one year.

Time deposits, another name for certificates of deposit or cds, are interest-bearing bank deposits that cannot be withdrawn without penalty before a specified date. Although time deposits may last for as long as five years, time deposits with terms of less than one year compete with other money-market instruments. Banks in the United States held $795 billion in large time deposits at the end of 1998.

International agency paper is issued by the World Bank, the Inter-American Development Bank and other organisations owned by member governments. These organisations often borrow in many different currencies. The World Bank, for example, had $6.7 billion in short-term debt outstanding at June 30th 1998, including notes denominated in Czech koruna, Italian lire, New Zealand dollars, Polish zlotys, South African rand and US dollars.

Repos. Repurchase agreements, known as repos, play a critical role in the money markets. They serve to keep the markets highly liquid, which in turn ensures that there will be a constant supply of buyers for new money-market instruments.

A repo is a combination of two transactions. In the first, a securities dealer, such as a bank, sells securities it owns to an investor, agreeing to repurchase the securities at a specified higher price at a future date. In the second transaction, days or months later, the repo is unwound as the dealer buys back the securities from the investor. The amount the investor lends is less than the market value of the securities, a difference called the haircut, to ensure that it still has sufficient collateral if the value of the securities should fall before the dealer repurchases them.

For the investor, the repo offers a profitable short-term use for unneeded cash. A large investor whose investment is greater than the amount covered by bank insurance may deem repos safer than bank deposits, as there is no risk of loss if the bank fails. The investor profits in two different ways. First, it receives more for reselling the securities than it paid to purchase them. In effect, it is collecting interest on the money it advances to the dealer at a rate known as the repo rate. Second, if it believes the price of the securities will fall the investor can sell them and later purchase equivalent securities to return to the dealer just before the repo must be unwound. The dealer, meanwhile, has obtained a loan in the cheapest possible way, and can use the proceeds to purchase yet more securities.

In a reverse repo the roles are switched, with an investor selling securities to a dealer and subsequently repurchasing them. The benefit to the investor is the use of cash at an interest rate below that of other instruments.

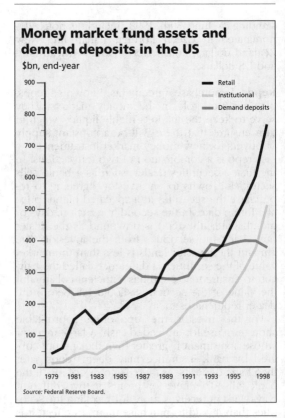

Money market fund assets and demand deposits in the US

$bn, end-year

Legend:
- Retail
- Institutional
- Demand deposits

Source: Federal Reserve Board.

Domestic money-market instruments worldwide ($bn, end-year)

	1993	1995	1996	1997	1998
Commercial paper	761.3	915.4	1,072.7	1,213.2	1,424.4
Treasury bills	1,771.2	2,109.6	1,965.4	1,814.0	1,836.3
Other short-term paper	1,146.9	1,584.5	1,610.6	1,650.0	1,870.7
Total	3,679.4	4,609.5	4,648.7	4,677.6	5,131.4

Source: Bank for International Settlements.

Commercial paper outstanding in the United States ($bn, seasonally adjusted, end-year)

	Financial	Non-financial	Total
1990	421	150	571
1991	403	133	535
1992	407	146	553
1993	407	154	562
1994	444	165	609
1995	497	190	687
1996	601	187	788
1997	766	201	967
1998	936	227	1,163

Source: Federal Reserve Board.

The UK market for commercial paper

Fourth quarter	Total (£bn)
1996	7.5
1997	9.5
1998	9.9

Source: Bank of England.

Short-term debt issuance by US government agencies

	$bn
1990	581.7
1991	717.5
1992	802.8
1993	1,233.6
1994	2,070.6
1995	3,280.4
1996	4,221.9
1997	5,406.4
1998	5,812.8

Source: Bond Market Association.

The US repo market, average daily amount outstanding ($bn)

	Repos	Reverse repos	Total
1981	65.4	46.7	112.1
1982	95.2	75.1	170.3
1983	102.4	81.7	184.1
1984	132.6	112.4	245.0
1985	172.9	147.9	320.8
1986	244.5	207.7	452.2
1987	292.0	275.0	567.0
1988	309.7	313.6	623.3
1989	398.2	383.2	781.4
1990	413.5	377.1	790.5
1991	496.6	417.0	913.6
1992	628.2	511.1	1,139.3
1993	765.6	594.1	1,359.7
1994	825.9	651.2	1,477.1
1995	821.5	618.8	1,440.3
1996	973.7	718.1	1,691.8
1997	1,159.0	883.0	2,042.0
1998	1,449.9	1,141.1	2,591.0

Source: Federal Reserve Bank of New York.

The UK repo market, amounts outstanding (£bn)

	Repos	Reverse repos	Total
February 1996	36.9	34.4	70.3
May 1996	34.7	33.7	68.4
August 1996	56.6	53.9	110.5
November 1996	68.6	60.3	128.9
February 1997	71.0	67.1	138.1
May 1997	79.6	71.3	150.9
August 1997	69.9	63.2	133.1
November 1997	72.3	70.6	142.9
February 1998	95.4	93.7	189.1
May 1998	76.3	69.1	145.4
August 1998	104.5	92.2	196.7

Source: Bank of England.

Size of repo markets (% of nominal GDP)

	1995	1997
Belgium	18.4	25.0
France	14.5	21.7
Italy	8.1	9.9
Japan	n/a	5.7
UK	0.0	9.5
US	12.0	14.9

Source: Bank for International Settlements.

Comparative interest rates
%, 1998

	Discount[a]	Money market	Deposit	Prime lending	Treasury bills	Gov't bonds
Australia	...	...	...	8.04	4.84	5.50
Austria	2.50	3.36	4.67	...	...	4.29
Belgium	2.75	3.58	2.65	7.25	3.51	4.72
Canada	5.25	5.11	5.03	6.60	4.73	5.47
Denmark	3.50	4.27	3.08	7.90	...	4.59
France	...	3.39	3.21	6.55	3.46	4.69
Germany	2.50	3.41	2.88	9.02	3.42	4.39
Italy	5.50	4.99	3.16	7.89	4.59	4.90
Japan	0.50	0.37	0.27	2.32	...	1.10
Netherlands	...	3.21	3.10	6.50	...	4.87
Spain	3.00	4.34	2.92	5.01	3.79	4.55
Sweden	2.00	4.24	1.91	5.94	4.19	...
Switzerland	1.00	1.22	0.69	4.07	1.32	2.39
UK	n.a.	7.09	4.48	7.21	6.82	5.45
US	4.50	5.35	5.47	8.35	4.82	5.26

a End-1998.
Source: IMF.

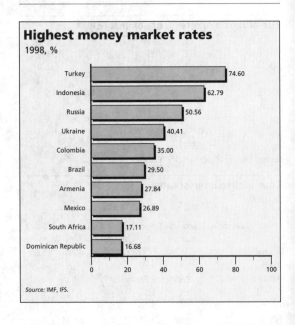

Highest money market rates
1998, %

Turkey	74.60
Indonesia	62.79
Russia	50.56
Ukraine	40.41
Colombia	35.00
Brazil	29.50
Armenia	27.84
Mexico	26.89
South Africa	17.11
Dominican Republic	16.68

0   20   40   60   80   100

Source: IMF, IFS.

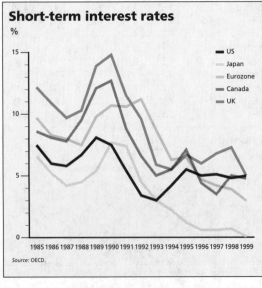

Short-term interest rates
%

- US
- Japan
- Eurozone
- Canada
- UK

15

10

5

0

1985 1986 1987 1988 1989 1990 1991 1992 1993 1994 1995 1996 1997 1998 1999

Source: OECD.

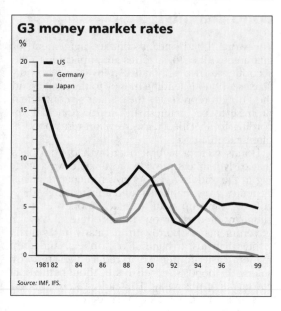

G3 money market rates
%

- US
- Germany
- Japan

Source: IMF, IFS.

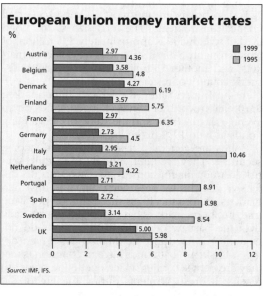

European Union money market rates
%

- 1999
- 1995

Country	1999	1995
Austria	2.97	4.36
Belgium	3.58	4.8
Denmark	4.27	6.19
Finland	3.57	5.75
France	2.97	6.35
Germany	2.73	4.5
Italy	2.95	10.46
Netherlands	3.21	4.22
Portugal	2.71	8.91
Spain	2.72	8.98
Sweden	3.14	8.54
UK	5.00	5.98

Source: IMF, IFS.

Bond markets

The word "bond" means contract, agreement, or guarantee. All of these terms are applicable to the securities known as bonds. An investor who purchases a bond is lending money to the issuer, and the bond represents the issuer's contractual promise to pay interest and repay principal according to specified terms. A short-term bond is often called a note.

Bonds were a natural outgrowth of the loans that early bankers provided to finance wars starting in the Middle Ages. As governments' financial appetites grew, bankers found it increasingly difficult to come up with as much money as their clients wanted to borrow. Bonds offered a way for governments to borrow from many individuals rather than just a handful of bankers, and they made it easier for lenders to reduce their risks by selling the bonds to others if they thought the borrower might not repay. The earliest known bond was issued by the Bank of Venice in 1157, to fund a war with Constantinople.

Today, bonds are the most widely used of all financial instruments. The total size of the bond market worldwide is approximately $34 trillion, of which roughly $29 trillion trades on domestic markets, and another $5 trillion trades outside the issuer's country of residence.

In the United States, the largest single market, $370 billion worth of bonds changed hands on an average day in 1998, and the value of outstanding bonds at June 1999 exceeded $14 trillion.

Bonds are generally classified as fixed-income securities. They are often thought of as dull, low-risk instruments for conservative investors, as defensive vehicles for preserving capital in unsettled markets. Before the 1970s these stereotypes were true, but bond markets have changed dramatically over the past two decades. Some bonds do not guarantee a fixed income. Many bear a high degree of risk. All that bonds have in common is that they are debt securities which entitle the owner to receive interest payments during the life of the bond and repayment of principal, without having ownership or managerial control of the issuer.

Types of bonds

An increasing variety of bonds is available in the marketplace. In some cases, an issuer agrees to design a bond with the specific characteristics required by a particular institutional investor. Such a bond is then privately placed and is not traded in the bond markets. Bonds that are issued in the public markets generally fit into one or more of the following categories.

Straight bonds. Also known as debentures, straight bonds are the basic fixed-income investment. The owner receives interest payments of a predetermined amount on specified dates, usually every six months or every year following the date of issue. The issuer must redeem the bond from the owner at its face value, known as the par value, on a specific date.

Callable bonds. The issuer may reserve the right to call the bonds at particular dates. A call obliges the owner to sell the bonds to the issuer for a price, specified when the bond was issued, that usually exceeds the current market price. The difference between the call price and the current market price is the call premium. A bond that is callable is worth less than an identical bond that is non-callable, to compensate the investor for the risk that it will not receive all of the anticipated interest payments.

Non-refundable bonds. These may be called only if the issuer is able to generate the funds internally, from sales or taxes. This prohibits an issuer from selling new bonds at a lower interest rate and using the proceeds to call bonds that bear a higher interest rate.

Putable bonds. Putable bonds give the investor the right to sell the bonds back to the issuer at par value on designated dates. This benefits the investor if interest rates rise, so a putable bond is worth more than an identical bond that is not putable.

Perpetual debentures. Also known as irredeemable debentures, perpetual debentures are bonds that will last forever unless the holder agrees to sell them back to the issuer.

Zero-coupon bonds. Zero-coupon bonds do not pay periodic interest. Instead, they are issued at less than par value and are redeemed at par value, with the difference serving as an interest payment. Zeros are designed to eliminate reinvestment risk, the loss an investor suffers if future income or principal payments from a bond must be invested at lower rates than those available today. The owner of a zero-coupon bond has no payments to reinvest until the bond matures, and therefore has greater certainty about the return on the investment.

Outstanding amounts of domestic debt securities, December 1998

Country	$trn
United States	13.8
Japan	5.2
Germany	2.0
Italy	1.6
France	1.2
UK	0.9
Canada	0.5
Belgium	0.4
Brazil	0.4
Spain	0.4

Source: Bank for International Settlements.

What bond ratings mean[a]

	Moody's	Standard & Poor's
Highest credit quality; issuer has strong ability to meet obligations	Aaa	AAA
Very high credit quality; low risk of default	Aa1	AA+
	Aa2	AA
	Aa3	AA−
High credit quality, but more vulnerable to changes in economy or business	A1	A+
	A2	A
	A3	A−
Adequate credit quality for now, but more likely to be impaired if conditions worsen	Baa1	BBB+
	Baa2	BBB
	Baa3	BBB−
Below investment grade, but good chance that issuer can meet commitments	Ba1	BB+
	Ba2	BB
	Ba3	BB−
Significant credit risk, but issuer is presently able to meet obligations	B1	B+
	B2	B
	B3	B−
High default risk	Caa1	CCC+
	Caa2	CCC
	Caa3	CCC−
Issuer failed to meet scheduled interest or principal payments	C	D

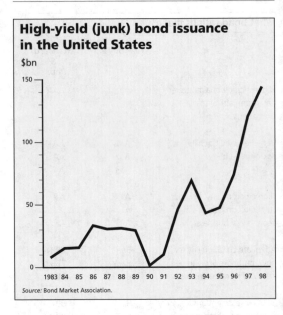

High-yield (junk) bond issuance in the United States

$bn

Source: Bond Market Association.

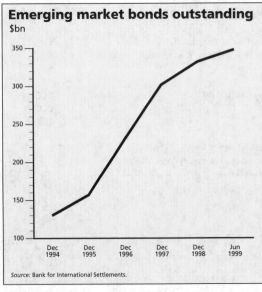

Emerging market bonds outstanding

$bn

Source: Bank for International Settlements.

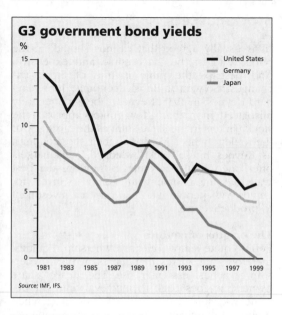

G3 government bond yields
%

— United States
— Germany
— Japan

15

10

5

0

1981 1983 1985 1987 1989 1991 1993 1995 1997 1999

Source: IMF, IFS.

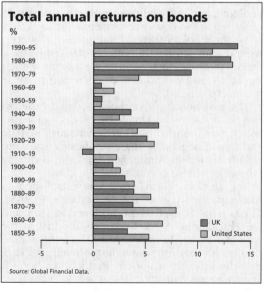

Total annual returns on bonds
%

1990–95
1980–89
1970–79
1960–69
1950–59
1940–49
1930–39
1920–29
1910–19
1900–09
1890–99
1880–89
1870–79
1860–69
1850–59

-5   0   5   10   15

■ UK
■ United States

Source: Global Financial Data.

Stockmarkets

"It is usually agreed that casinos should, in the public interest, be inaccessible and expensive. And perhaps the same is true of Stock Exchanges." So wrote a British economist, John Maynard Keynes, in 1935. Keynes's jibe is not entirely misplaced; more than a few punters approach the stockmarkets in the same spirit as the racetrack or the roulette wheel. Yet for all their shortcomings, as Keynes himself acknowledged, stockmarkets offer one singular advantage: they are the best way to bring people with money to invest together with people who can put that investment to productive use.

The origins of equities

Equity, quite simply, means ownership. Equities, therefore, are shares that represent part ownership of a business enterprise. The idea of share ownership goes back to medieval times. It became widespread during the Renaissance, when groups of merchants joined to finance trading expeditions and early bankers took part ownership of businesses to ensure repayment of loans. These early shareholder-owned enterprises, however, were usually temporary ventures established for a limited purpose, such as financing a single voyage by a ship, and were dissolved once their purpose was accomplished.

The first ongoing shareholder-owned business may have been the Dutch East India Company, which was founded by Dutch merchants in 1602 and issued negotiable share certificates that were readily traded in Amsterdam until the company failed almost two centuries later.

The first stock exchange was established in Antwerp, then part of the Netherlands, in 1631. The London Stock Exchange opened in 1773, and the Philadelphia Stock Exchange, the first in the New World, began trading in 1790. By the middle of the 19th century, with industry hungry for capital, almost every major city had its own bourse. Britain alone had 20 different stock exchanges.

This was necessary because most listed firms were unknown outside their home region and so preferred to list their shares locally, and most investors were individuals who preferred to buy the shares of firms that they knew.

Many of these exchanges disappeared as capital markets became national and then international. Now most countries (the United States being the main exception) have a single dominant stock exchange. It is increasingly common for companies to list their shares on foreign exchanges as well as domestically, giving them access to a wider array of investors. International equity issues (shares issued outside the issuing company's home country) were rare at the beginning of the 1990s, but they have increased substantially in recent years.

The biggest exchanges

The overwhelming majority of the world's equity trading takes place on just four exchanges: the New York Stock Exchange; the NASDAQ stockmarkets (formerly known as the National Association of Securities Dealers Automated Quotation System); the Tokyo Stock Exchange; and the London Stock Exchange. The New York Stock Exchange is by far the largest as measured by market capitalisation, listing shares whose total value exceeded $11 trillion at the end of 1999. NASDAQ had a market capitalisation of over $5 trillion (but was hit by the fall in tech stocks in 2000). Tokyo Stock Exchange, which lost its status as the world's largest with the dramatic decline in Japanese share prices, was valued at nearly $4.5 trillion and London was nearly $3 trillion.

Until the late 1990s almost every firm listed its shares exclusively on a stock exchange in its home country. Investors, particularly pension funds and insurance companies whose liabilities were entirely in their home country, preferred to own assets denominated in that same currency. Today, however, many multinational firms list their shares on major exchanges in North America and Europe (see chart on page 129).

Largest stockmarket capitalisation
$m, end 1998

1	United States	13,451,352		21	India	105,188
2	Japan	2,495,757		22	Denmark	98,881
3	United Kingdom	2,374,273		23	Malaysia	98,557
4	Germany	1,093,962		24	Singapore	94,469
5	France	991,484		25	Mexico	91,746
6	Australia	874,283		26	New Zealand	89,373
7	Switzerland	689,199		27	Greece	79,992
8	Netherlands	603,182		28	Portugal	62,954
9	Italy	569,731		29	Norway	56,285
10	Canada	543,394		30	Chile	51,866
11	Spain	402,180		31	Argentina	45,332
12	Hong Kong	343,394		32	Saudi Arabia	42,563
13	Sweden	278,707		33	Israel	39,628
14	Taiwan	260,015		34	Luxembourg	35,403
15	Belgium	245,657		35	Philippines	35,314
16	China	231,322		36	Thailand	34,903
17	South Africa	170,252		37	Austria	34,106
18	Brazil	160,887		38	Turkey	33,646
19	Finland	154,518		39	Ireland	29,956
20	South Korea	114,593		40	Egypt	24,381

Highest growth in market capitalisation, $ terms
% increase, 1989–98

1	China	11,306		18	Barbados	755
2	Russia[a]	9,349		19	Panama[c]	699
3	Poland[a]	9,117		20	Slovenia[b]	688
4	Morocco	2,424		21	Lithuania[b]	584
5	Hungary[a]	2,396		22	Paraguay[e]	578
6	Ghana[a]	1,548		23	New Zealand	563
7	Bulgaria[b]	1,526		24	Australia	520
8	Namibia[c]	1,432		25	Armenia[b]	500
9	Egypt	1,325		26	Lebanon[b]	496
10	Greece	1,155		27	Portugal	493
11	Peru	1,151		28	Bolivia[b]	488
12	Colombia	1,076		29	Croatia[b]	449
13	Argentina	973		30	Chile	441
14	Romania[b]	916		31	Venezuela	415
15	Indonesia	881		32	Finland	404
16	Trinidad & Tobago	854		33	Turkey	396
17	Mauritius[d]	768		34	Israel	382

Highest growth in value traded, $ terms
% increase, 1989–98

1	Romania[b]	59,100		21	Panama[c]	1,386
2	Hungary[a]	42,361		22	China[a]	1,384
3	Bangladesh	15,760		23	Russia[b]	1,363
4	Morocco	8,556		24	Italy	1,122
5	Turkey	8,502		25	Ghana[c]	1,100
6	Greece	8,461		26	Sweden	1,069
7	Egypt	5,425		27	Luxembourg	1,007
8	Poland[a]	5,242		28	Switzerland[d]	826
9	Pakistan	4,616		29	Australia	810
10	Nigeria	3,925		30	Brazil	775
11	Sri Lanka	3,914		31	South Africa	724
12	Peru	2,984		32	Finland	719
13	Portugal	2,388		33	Argentina	687
14	Colombia	1,980		34	Cote d'Ivoire	680
15	Mauritius[d]	1,940		35	Cyprus[a]	620
16	Spain	1,721		36	Belgium	618
17	Oman[c]	1,699			Kenya	618
18	Indonesia	1,695		38	United States	502
19	New Zealand	1,569		39	Bolivia[b]	500
20	Venezuela	1,524			Lithuania[b]	500

Highest growth in number of listed companies
% increase, 1989–98

1	Romania[b]	82,086		16	India	143
2	Slovakia[b]	4,550		17	Taiwan	141
3	Bulgaria[b]	3,738		18	Hungary[a]	139
4	China[a]	1,540			Thailand	139
5	Poland[a]	1,138		20	Singapore	136
6	Russia[a]	812		21	Hong Kong	132
7	Paraguay[e]	511		22	Fiji[b]	125
8	Turkey	454		23	Tunisia[c]	124
9	Indonesia	404		24	Honduras[a]	114
10	Namibia[c]	275		25	Iceland[b]	107
11	Malaysia	193		26	Greece	105
12	Oman	152			Iran[a]	105
13	Swaziland[d]	150		28	Bolivia[b]	100
14	Israel	148			Mauritius[d]	100
15	Panama[c]	145		30	Colombia	99

a 1992–98   b 1995–98   c 1993–98   d 1991–98   e 1994–98

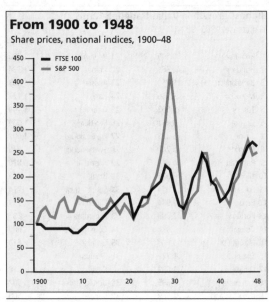

From 1900 to 1948

Share prices, national indices, 1900–48

- FTSE 100
- S&P 500

Returns on stocks

Annual average, %

	United States	UK
1850–59	0.45	5.18
1860–69	15.76	4.48
1870–79	7.58	5.28
1880–89	6.72	5.56
1890–99	5.45	3.02
1900–09	9.62	0.48
1910–19	4.69	2.24
1920–29	13.86	7.23
1930–39	−0.17	1.94
1940–49	9.57	8.89
1950–59	18.23	17.18
1960–69	8.17	8.30
1970–79	6.75	10.12
1980–89	16.64	23.72
1990–95	13.00	11.73

Source: Global Financial Data.

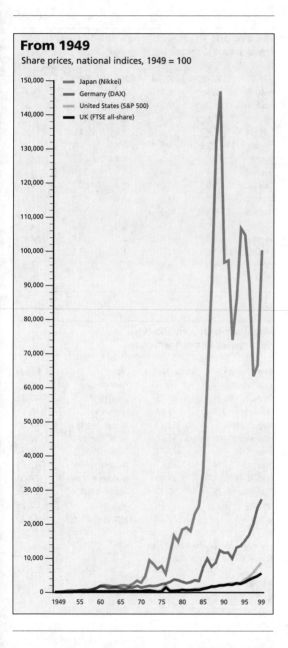

From 1949

Share prices, national indices, 1949 = 100

Japan (Nikkei)
Germany (DAX)
United States (S&P 500)
UK (FTSE all-share)

Share prices
Annual average % change

	1985–89	1990–94	1995	1998	1999
Australia	15.3	8.4	-1.4	4.6	11.4
Austria	15.0	-7.0	-13.4	12.8	n.a.
Belgium	17.8	3.3	-6.1	53.2	n.a.
Canada	8.8	5.8	3.5	4.6	4.5
Denmark	7.2	4.9	-0.8	8.0	-11.4
France	23.8	5.1	-8.9	34.9	24.0
Germany	7.4	1.4	8.5	28.0	3.7
Italy	19.0	1.0	-8.4	60.1	n.a.
Japan	26.7	-7.5	-13.6	-15.5	17.6
Netherlands	8.2	10.3	8.1	33.9	8.8
Spain	37.0	3.0	-5.9	47.0	7.0
Sweden	31.6	7.4	12.0	15.8	18.1
Switzerland	9.8	12.3	1.1	33.2	1.7
UK	15.3	8.6	4.1	17.3	12.3
USA	15.5	8.4	18.9	24.7	26.5

Source: IMF.

Major world[a] stockmarkets
Best and worst 12-month performance

Best	% gain	Worst	% loss
Year ending		Year ending	
February 1934	84.13	June 1932	-47.85
November 1933	71.74	December 1931	-41.08
August 1986	62.41	September 1974	40.49
January 1987	53.26	November 1920	-32.11
June 1983	42.77	March 1938	-26.36
December 1954	38.33	August 1930	-25.63
August 1959	37.11	November 1946	-24.01
December 1985	37.02	September 1990	-22.98
January 1955	36.70	May 1970	-22.56
June 1971	31.16	March 1921	-22.15

a Western Europe and North America.
Source: Global Financial Data.

Major world[a] stockmarkets
Best and worse monthly performance

Best	% gain	Worst	% loss
May 1933	14.94	September 1931	-18.16
January 1975	14.27	October 1987	-17.12
April 1933	13.93	January 1946	-16.51
August 1932	13.73	November 1973	-13.15
January 1987	11.57	December 1931	-11.65
July 1989	11.13	March 1980	-11.06
May 1990	10.33	May 1940	-10.82
July 1933	9.85	September 1990	-10.75
August 1984	9.76	October 1944	-10.61
March 1986	9.56	August 1974	-10.21
July 1932	9.36	October 1929	-10.00

Source: Global Financial Data.

US shares
Best and worst 12-month performance

Best	% gain	Worst	% loss
Year ending		*Year ending*	
June 1933	146.28	June 1932	-70.13
February 1934	90.11	March 1938	-52.57
March 1936	76.15	September 1931	-47.77
May 1863	73.00	October 1857	-42.65
October 1862	61.54	September 1974	-41.40
Janaury 1934	60.95	December 1937	-38.60
April 1844	54.67	September 1930	-38.36
October 1860	54.17	November 1907	-37.06
August 1929	51.94	June 1877	-34.13
July 1983	51.80	February 1933	-31.72

a Western Europe and North America.
Source: Global Financial Data.

US shares
Best and worst daily performance, Dow Jones Industrial Average

Best	% Gain	Worst	% Loss
March 15 1933	15.34	October 19 1987	-22.61
October 6 1931	14.87	October 28 1929	-13.47
October 30 1929	12.84	October 29 1929	-11.73
June 22 1931	11.90	October 5 1931	-10.73
September 21 1932	11.36	November 6 1929	-9.92
October 21 1987	10.15	December 18 1899	-8.73
August 3 1932	9.52	August 12 1932	-8.40
September 5 1939	9.52	March 14 1907	-8.29
February 11 1932	9.47	January 4 1932	-8.10
November 14 1929	9.36	October 26 1987	-8.04

Source: Global Financial Data.

UK shares
Best and worst daily performance

Best	% Gain	Worst	% Loss
September 23 1931	12.81	October 20 1987	-11.66
January 24 1975	10.09	October 19 1987	-10.13
September 29 1938	8.41	March 1 1974	-7.10
July 1 1975	8.12	January 2 1975	-6.69
February 10 1975	7.44	May 29 1962	-6.44
January 30 1975	7.36	October 26 1987	-6.42
April 17 1975	6.99	February 17 1975	-6.21
February 7 1975	6.69	January 31 1975	-6.10
February 26 1976	6.20	October 22 1987	-6.02
March 30 1971	6.18	March 17 1975	-5.75

Source: Global Financial Data.

German shares
Best and worst daily performance since 1955

Best	% Gain	Worst	% Loss
May 30 1962	13.09	October 16 1989	-13.47
May 29 1970	8.70	August 19 1991	-10.34
October 29 1962	7.57	May 29 1962	-7.35
October 30 1987	6.93	November 10 1987	-7.31
October 17 1989	6.92	October 19 1987	-7.06
November 12 1987	6.70	November 9 1987	-6.38
October 21 1987	6.64	October 26 1987	-5.63
August 7 1967	5.62	March 6 1961	-5.38
October 1 1990	5.56	January 28 1987	-5.35
August 27 1990	5.50	April 28 1970	-5.28

Source: Global Financial Data.

Japanese shares
Best and worst daily performance since 1953

Best	% Gain	Worst	% Loss
October 2 1990	9.54	October 20 1987	-14.63
October 21 1987	9.39	March 5 1953	-8.75
August 21 1992	7.56	April 30 1970	-7.47
April 10 1992	7.22	April 2 1990	-7.10
January 3 1994	6.64	August 16 1971	-5.75
January 6 1988	6.57	August 23 1990	-5.70
April 6 1953	6.39	August 19 1991	-5.24
March 6 1953	5.38	November 29 1993	-5.20
December 1 1993	5.07	June 24 1972	-5.20
July 7 1995	5.03	August 19 1971	-5.18

Source: Global Financial Data.

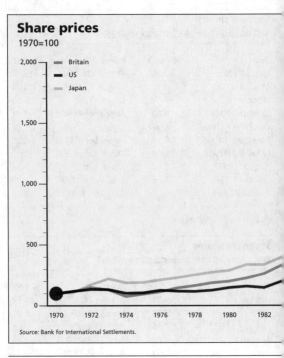

Share prices
1970=100

Legend:
- Britain
- US
- Japan

Source: Bank for International Settlements.

Share price indicators
Price/earnings ratios

	Starting date	Peak level	Peak year	Average
United States	1957	27	1998	16
Japan	1981	100	1996	51
Germany	1973	25	1993	13
France	1973	30	1973	12
Italy	1986	29	1994	17
United Kingdom	1970	23	1994	13
Canada	1956	255	1994	20
Belgium	1961	29	1967	16
Netherlands	1973	26	1997	10
Switzerland	1973	29	1998	13

Source: Bank for International Settlements.

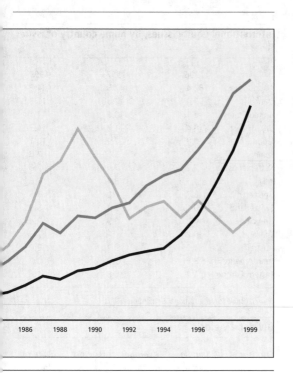

Starting date	Trough level	Trough date	Average
1947	1.5	1998	4.0
1953	0.4	1989	3.0
1973	1.3	1998	2.8
1964	1.7	1998	4.5
1981	0.8	1981	2.3
1963	2.8	1998	4.7
1956	1.4	1998	3.4
1961	1.6	1998	4.3
1973	1.8	1998	4.8
1973	1.0	1995	2.9

International equity issues, by home country of issuer
$bn

	1996	1997	1998
All countries	82.4	117.5	124.2
France	7.4	12.6	17.3
United States	8.1	8.9	17.1
UK	8.4	11.7	14.3
Japan	0.8	1.9	10.1
Spain	1.7	5.0	7.6
Netherlands	7.2	7.0	7.6
Italy	4.5	8.4	7.6
Germany	8.7	6.0	7.5
Switzerland	0.1	3.4	5.9
Greece	0.2	0.9	2.4
Thailand	0.2	–	2.3
Australia	1.2	3.2	2.0
Latin America	3.5	5.9	0.2
Eastern Europe	1.2	2.8	1.6

Source: Bank for International Settlements.

Dividend yields

Country	Sample began	Average dividend (%)	Lowest annual dividend (%)	Date of lowest dividend
Belgium	1961	4.3	1.6	1998
Canada	1956	3.4	1.4	1998
France	1964	4.5	1.7	1998
Germany	1973	2.8	1.3	1998
Italy	1981	2.3	0.8	1981
Japan	1953	3.0	0.4	1989
Netherlands	1973	4.8	1.8	1998
Switzerland	1973	2.9	1.0	1995
UK	1963	4.7	2.8	1998
United States	1947	4.0	1.5	1998

Source: Bank for International Settlements.

Initial public offerings in US markets[a]

Year	Number	Value $m
1989	182	6,115
1990	158	4,627
1991	380	16,350
1992	528	29,359
1993	628	38,524
1994	539	31,619
1995	557	31,770
1996	786	36,956
1997	604	38,449
1998	362	49,992

a On NYSE, NASDAQ, AMEX.
Source: NASD.

Secondary offerings in US markets[a]

Year	Number	Value $m
1991	436	29,626
1992	442	32,203
1993	583	48,139
1994	386	33,647
1995	535	55,064
1996	616	57,012
1997	544	58,924
1998	495	68,823

a On NYSE, NASDAQ, AMEX.
Source: NASD.

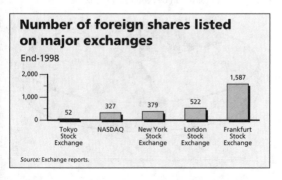

Number of foreign shares listed on major exchanges

End-1998

- Tokyo Stock Exchange: 52
- NASDAQ: 327
- New York Stock Exchange: 379
- London Stock Exchange: 522
- Frankfurt Stock Exchange: 1,587

Source: Exchange reports.

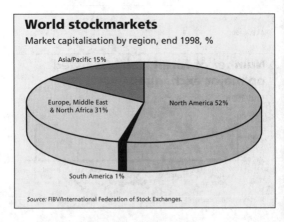

Largest stockmarkets

Market capitalisation, end 1999, $bn

% change

1	Nasdaq	132	7	Italy	28.7
2	Tokyo	82.6	8	London	20.3
3	Hong Kong	77.3	9	Amsterdam	15.8
4	Paris	52.6	10	New York	11.3
5	Toronto	45.2	11	Switzerland	-1.2
6	Germany	31.8			

New York 11,437.6
Nasdaq 5,204.6
Tokyo 4,455.3
London 2,855.4
Paris 1,503.0
Germany 1,432.2
Toronto 789.2
Italy 728.2
Amsterdam 695.2
Switzerland 693.1
Hong Kong 609.1

0   2,000   4,000   6,000   8,000   10,000   12,000

World stockmarkets

Market capitalisation by region, end 1998, %

Asia/Pacific 15%

Europe, Middle East & North Africa 31%

North America 52%

South America 1%

Source: FIBV/International Federation of Stock Exchanges.

Derivatives and options

The simple principle of market economics, that prices serve to bring supply and demand into balance, is familiar to everyone. But although markets for most things work well most of the time, on some occasions they work quite badly. Petroleum prices may soar, hurting airlines that have already sold tickets and now must pay much more than expected to operate their jets. The Australian dollar may suddenly drop against the yen, leaving an importer in Melbourne stuck with a shipload of Japanese electronic equipment that will be prohibitively expensive to sell. A German bank may unexpectedly report that a big borrower has defaulted, and its falling share price could cause a painful loss for an investment fund that had favoured its shares. The name for such price movements is volatility.

To a lay person volatility seems random and unpredictable. In truth, individual price movements usually are random and unpredictable. Yet over time average volatility can be measured, the probability of price movements can be estimated, and investors can determine how much they are willing to pay to reduce the amount of volatility they face. The derivatives market is where this occurs.

The term derivatives refers to a large number of financial instruments whose value is based on, or derived from, the prices of securities, commodities, money or other external variables. They come in hundreds of varieties. For all their diversity, however, they fall into two basic categories.

- Forwards are contracts that set a price for something to be delivered in the future.
- Options are contracts that allow, but do not require, one or both parties to obtain certain benefits under certain conditions. The calculation of an option contract's value must take into account the possibility that this option will be exercised.

All derivatives contracts are either forwards or options, or some combination of the two.

Derivatives have come to public attention only in the past few years, largely because of a series of spectacular losses from derivatives trading. Under various labels, however, derivatives contracts have been employed for thousands of years. The earliest known use was by a Greek philosopher, Thales, who reached individual agreements with the owners of olive presses whereby, in return for a payment, he obtained the right to first use of each owner's press after harvest. These options on all his region's pressing capacity, Aristotle reports, gave Thales control over the olive crop. Derivatives have been traded privately ever since, and have been bought and sold on exchanges since at least the 1600s.

Derivatives disasters

Derivatives have made it possible for firms and government agencies to manage their risks to an extent unimaginable only a decade ago. But derivatives are far from riskless. Used carelessly, they can increase risks in ways that users often fail to understand. As individual derivatives can be quite complex and difficult to comprehend, they have been blamed for a series of highly publicised financial disasters. In some cases, the dealers have been accused of selling products that were not suited to the users' needs. In other situations, the problem has been not with the instruments themselves, but with the financial controls of the organisation trading or using them. Here are some examples of the involvement of derivatives in big losses for companies, organisations and even countries.

Metallgesellschaft, a large German company with a big oil-trading operation, reported a $1.9 billion loss in 1993 on its positions in oil futures and swaps. The company was seeking to hedge contracts to supply petrol, heating oil and other products to customers. But its hedge, like most hedges, was not perfect, and declines in oil prices caused its derivative position to lose value more rapidly than its contracts to deliver oil in future gained value. The company's directors may have compounded the loss by ordering that the hedge be unwound, or sold off, before it was scheduled to expire.

Procter & Gamble, a large American consumer-products company, and Gibson Greetings, a manufacturer of greeting cards, announced huge losses from derivatives trading in April 1994. Both companies had purchased highly levered derivatives known as ratio swaps, based on formulas such as

$$\text{Net payment} = 5.5\% - \frac{\text{Libor}^2}{6\%}$$

If the resulting number is positive, the dealer must make a payment to the user. As interest rates rose early in 1994, however, the numerator rose geometrically, drastically increasing the users' losses. Procter & Gamble admitted to losing $157m, and Gibson's loss was about $20m. Both firms recovered part of their losses from the dealer, Bankers Trust Company. In both cases, the firms' derivative investments were made in violation of their own investment policies.

Barings, a venerable British investment bank, collapsed in February 1995 as a result of a loss of $1.47 billion on exchange-traded options on Japan's Nikkei 225 share index. Investigation subsequently revealed that the bank's management had exercised lax oversight of its trading position and had violated standard securities-industry procedures by allowing a staff member in Singapore, Nick Leeson, to both trade options and oversee the processing of his own trades, which enabled him to obscure his activities. Mr Leeson subsequently served a prison term in Singapore

Orange County, California, suffered a loss ultimately reckoned to be $1.69 billion after Robert Citron, the county's treasurer and manager of its investment fund, borrowed through repurchase agreements in order to speculate on lower interest rates. In the end, about $8 billion of a fund totalling $20 billion was invested in interest-sensitive derivatives such as inverse floaters, which magnify the gains or losses from interest-rate changes. These derivatives were designed to stop paying interest if market interest rates rose beyond a certain point. This large position was unhedged, and when the Federal Reserve raised interest rates six times within a nine-month period in 1994 the value of the fund's assets collapsed.

Sumitomo, a Japanese trading company, announced total losses of ¥330 billion ($3 billion) from derivatives transactions undertaken by its former chief copper trader, Yasuo Hamanaka. Mr Hamanaka, known for being one of the leading traders in the copper futures and options markets, was accused of having used fraud and forgery to conceal losses from his employer, while continuing to trade in an effort to recoup the losses. Inadequate financial controls apparently allowed the problems to mount unnoticed for a decade. After Sumitomo's huge losses were revealed in 1996, Mr Hamanaka was convicted and sentenced to a prison term.

Derivatives played a role in the financial crisis that crippled Thailand in the summer of 1997. Many investors misjudged the country's situation because the Thai central bank reported holding large foreign currency reserves. The central bank did not report that most of these reserves were committed to forward contracts intended to support the currency, the baht. Once the baht's market value fell, the bank suffered huge losses on its derivatives and its reserves were wiped out. A year later several American and European banks reported significant derivatives losses in Russia after a sharp fall in the country's currency led to the failure of several banks and caused local counterparties to derivatives trades to default.

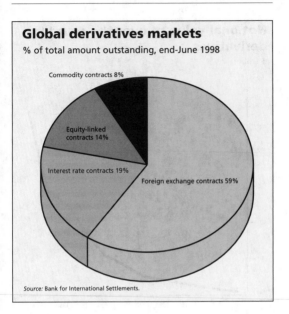

Global derivatives markets

% of total amount outstanding, end-June 1998

Commodity contracts 8%

Equity-linked contracts 14%

Interest rate contracts 19%

Foreign exchange contracts 59%

Source: Bank for International Settlements.

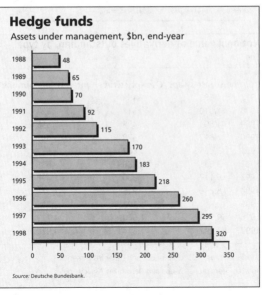

Hedge funds

Assets under management, $bn, end-year

Year	Value
1988	48
1989	65
1990	70
1991	92
1992	115
1993	170
1994	183
1995	218
1996	260
1997	295
1998	320

Source: Deutsche Bundesbank.

DERIVATIVES AND OPTIONS 135

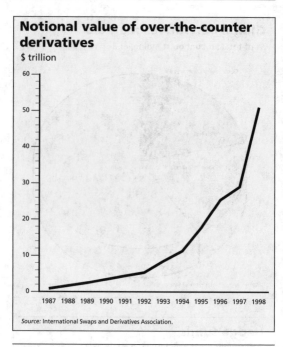

Notional value of over-the-counter derivatives
$ trillion

Source: International Swaps and Derivatives Association.

Notional value of derivatives outstanding, by type
$bn

	Interest-rate swaps	Currency swaps	Interest-rate options[a]
1987	683	183	–
1988	1,010	317	327
1989	1,503	435	538
1990	2,312	578	561
1991	3,065	807	577
1992	3,851	860	635
1993	6,117	900	1,398
1994	8,816	915	1,573
1995	12,811	1,197	3,705
1996	19,171	1,560	4,723
1997	22,291	1,824	4,920

a Includes caps, floors, swaptions and other instruments.
Source: International Swaps and Derivatives Association.

Banking

Largest banks
By capital, $m

1	Citicorp	United States	41,889
2	BankAmerica Corp	United States	36,887
3	HSBC Holdings	United Kingdom	29,352
4	Crédit Agricole	France	25,930
5	Chase Manhattan Corp	United States	24,121
6	Industrial and Commercial Bank of China	China	22,213
7	Bank of Tokyo-Mitsubishi	Japan	22,074
8	UBS	Switzerland	20,525
9	Sakura Bank	Japan	19,899
10	Bank One Corp	United States	19,654
11	Fuji Bank	Japan	19,590
12	Deutsche Bank	Germany	18,680
13	Sanwa Bank	Japan	17,745
14	Credit Suisse Group	Switzerland	17,579
15	ABN-Amro Bank	Netherlands	17,471
16	Dai-Ichi Kangyo Bank	Japan	17,234
17	Sumitomo Bank	Japan	16,220
18	Bank of China	China	14,712
19	Rabobank Nederland	Netherlands	14,688
20	Industrial Bank of Japan	Japan	14,529
21	First Union Corp	United States	13,592
22	Barclays Bank	United Kingdom	13,495
23	National Westminster Bank	United Kingdom	13,389
24	Tokai Bank	Japan	13,274
25	Dresdner Bank	Germany	13,042
26	ING Bank Group	Netherlands	12,961
27	Banque Nationale de Paris	France	12,824
28	Norinchukin Bank	Japan	12,585
29	Société Générale	France	12,521
30	Wells Fargo & Co	United States	12,424
31	Lloyds TSB Group	United Kingdom	12,111
32	Hypo-Vereinsbank	Germany	11,853
33	Commerzbank	Germany	11,760
34	Halifax	United Kingdom	11,564
35	J.P. Morgan & Co	United States	11,242
36	Crédit Mutuel	France	10,737

Notes: Capital is essentially equity and reserves.
Figures for Japanese banks refer to the year ended March 31, 1999. Figures for all other countries refer to the year ended December 31, 1998.

Institutional investment

Financial assets of institutional investors
% of GDP, 1996

	Insurance companies	Pension funds	Investment companies	Others
Australia	38.6	30.4	11.8	7.1
Belgium	30.9	4.1	25.9	5.1
Canada	29.7	40.7	24.3	n.a.
France	45.8	n.a.	37.2	n.a.
Germany	29.5	2.8	17.6	n.a.
Italy	12.0	3.2	10.6	28.3
Japan	37.9	n.a.	9.8	68.9
Netherlands	56.6	93.3	16.8	n.a.
Spain	18.6	2.0	24.8	n.a.
Sweden	56.9	2.4	23.9	70.3
UK	88.6	77.5	27.0	n.a.
United States	40.9	64.4	45.7	52.0

Source: OECD.

Foreign direct investment

Direct investment flows

	Inflows		Outflows	
	1995	1998	1995	1998
Developed countries	63.4	71.5	85.3	91.6
Western Europe	37.0	36.9	48.9	62.6
European Union	35.1	35.7	44.7	59.5
United States	17.9	30	25.7	20.5
Japan	nil	0.5	6.3	3.7
Developing countries	32.3	25.8	14.5	8.1
Africa	1.3	1.2	0.1	0.1
Western Hemisphere	10.0	11.1	2.1	2.4
Developing Europe	0.1	0.2	nil	nil
Asia	20.7	13.2	12.3	5.6
The Pacific	0.2	nil	nil	nil
Central and Eastern Europe	4.3	2.7	0.1	0.3

Source: United Nations Conference on Trade and Development.

The cashless world

Cashless transactions
% of total value of cashless transactions, 1997

	Cheques	Cards	Transfers	Direct debits
Belgium	2.9	0.2	96.6	0.3
Canada	97.1	0.8	1.5	0.6
France	4.4	0.2	93.3	1.0
Germany	1.6	nil	95.9	2.5
Italy	3.2	0.1	95.4	0.3
Japan	...	...	...	...
Netherlands	nil	0.2	98.8	1.0
Sweden	...	1.7	95.8	2.5
Switzerland	...	0.1	99.8	0.1
UK	4.2	0.3	94.6	1.0
United States	10.5	0.2	88.5	0.8

Source: Bank for International Settlements.

Cash dispensers
1998

	Machines per 1,000,000 population	Transactions per inhabitant	Average transaction value $
Belgium	492	15.7	114.3
Canada	645	52.7	50.4
France	461	19.9	68.0
Germany	504	...	...
Italy	443	7.2	184.7
Japan	1,115	5.0	288.8
Netherlands	409	33.3	87.9
Sweden	268	35.3	104.5
Switzerland	678	11.4	186.6
UK	393	29.6	84.5
United States	616	40.7	68.3

Source: Bank for International Settlements.

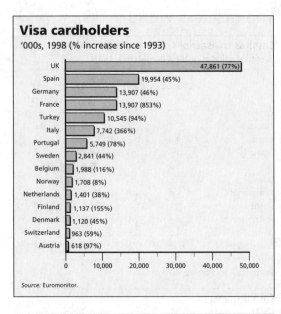

Visa cardholders

'000s, 1998 (% increase since 1993)

UK	47,861 (77%)
Spain	19,954 (45%)
Germany	13,907 (46%)
France	13,907 (853%)
Turkey	10,545 (94%)
Italy	7,742 (366%)
Portugal	5,749 (78%)
Sweden	2,841 (44%)
Belgium	1,988 (116%)
Norway	1,708 (8%)
Netherlands	1,401 (38%)
Finland	1,137 (155%)
Denmark	1,120 (45%)
Switzerland	963 (59%)
Austria	618 (97%)

0   10,000   20,000   30,000   40,000   50,000

Source: Euromonitor.

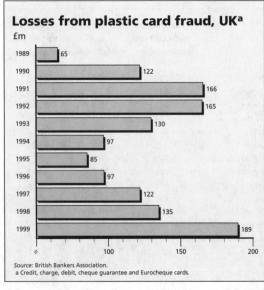

Losses from plastic card fraud, UK[a]

£m

1989	65
1990	122
1991	166
1992	165
1993	130
1994	97
1995	85
1996	97
1997	122
1998	135
1999	189

100   150   200

Source: British Bankers Association.
a Credit, charge, debit, cheque guarantee and Eurocheque cards.

Plastic card fraud losses of UK issuers[a]
£m

	1991	1992	1993	1994	1995	1996	1997
Total	165.6	165.0	129.8	96.8	83.3	97.1	122.0
By card type							
Credit cards	81.2	76.7	57.6	43.5	38.3	43.7	60.4
Charge cards	16.4	16.2	13.9	11.6	10.0	14.2	16.6
Debit cards	35.4	43.9	35.8	23.9	20.0	25.4	33.9
Cheque guarantee cards[b]	29.9	25.6	20.6	16.4	13.8	12.8	10.4
Eurocheque cards	2.7	2.6	1.9	1.4	1.2	1.0	0.7
By circumstances of card loss							
Cards reported lost or stolen	124.1	123.2	98.5	71.1	60.1	60.0	66.2
Cards not received by card holder	32.9	29.6	18.2	12.6	9.1	10.0	12.5
Counterfeit card	4.6	8.4	9.9	9.6	7.7	13.3	20.3
Other	4.0	3.7	3.3	3.7	6.4	13.7	23.1
By place of misuse							
ATM transactions	3.7	3.4	2.5	3.2	3.5	4.4	8.2
Card withdrawals at bank counter	8.6	8.6	6.7	5.0	4.8	3.9	4.3
Card not-present transactions	0.4	1.0	1.3	2.2	4.3	6.0	8.2
Other merchant transactions[c]	127.9	130.2	95.8	65.5	49.5	57.3	72.2
Total transactions							
in UK	140.6	143.2	106.4	75.9	62.1	71.6	92.9
abroad	25.0	21.8	23.4	21.0	21.2	25.4	29.2

Source: Association of Payment Clearing Services (APACS)

a Relate to cards issued in the UK only and cover losses worldwide. Losses on single-function ATM cards orforeign-issued cards used in the UK are not included.

b Include losses on multi-function cards when used to guarantee personal cheques.

c Merchants are retailers and all other service providers authorised to accept plastic cards.

Web sales worldwide
$ bn

	Business to consumer	Total
1998	8	50
1999	20	80
2000	45	190
2001	90	330
2002	180	590
2003	220	900
2004	300	1400

Note: 2000 to 2004 are forecasts.
Source: Keenan Vision.

EIU e-business readiness rankings, spring 2000

Top five	Score	Bottom five	Score
United States	8.8	Iraq	2.0
Sweden	8.3	Nigeria	3.3
Finland	8.6	Iran	3.3
Norway	8.5	Algeria	3.5
Netherlands	8.4	Kazakhstan	3.5

Source: The EIU ebusiness forum.

European e-commerce markets
$ m

	1997	2001 forecast
Germany	73	3,230
Britain	9	1,410
France	4	712
Netherlands	2	416
Sweden	3	142
Italy	1	118
Spain	1	93

Source: Datamonitor.

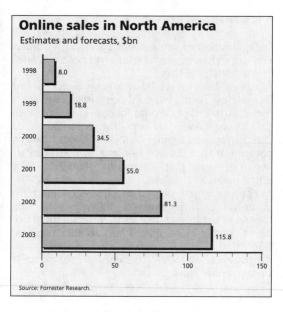

Online sales in North America
Estimates and forecasts, $bn

Year	Value
1998	8.0
1999	18.8
2000	34.5
2001	55.0
2002	81.3
2003	115.8

Source: Forrester Research.

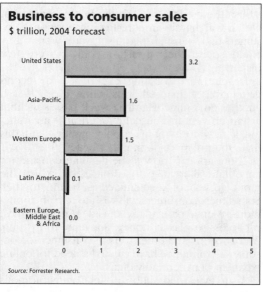

Business to consumer sales
$ trillion, 2004 forecast

United States	3.2
Asia-Pacific	1.6
Western Europe	1.5
Latin America	0.1
Eastern Europe, Middle East & Africa	0.0

Source: Forrester Research.

Virtual money

Digital currencies are sprouting all over the Internet. But virtual money does not yet pose a serious threat to the real thing

Money has always been a sexy topic. As has technology. So the hype that greeted the arrival in the mid-1990s of several digital kinds of cash should not have been surprising. Some predicted that private electronic currencies would swiftly compete with dollars or D-marks. Central bankers began to worry that – perish the thought! – they might become obsolete.

The reality has proved much less exciting: for electronic cash has flopped badly. Its issuers either went bankrupt (DigiCash), dropped the product (CyberCash) or moved into another business (First Virtual Holdings, now MessageMedia). On the Internet, almost all payments are still made by unsexy credit cards.

In fact, digital cash was always a long shot. Around the world, money brings out a conservative streak. Even in America, it took decades to establish the credit card. And the first generation of e-cash was hardly an attractive proposition. Consumers had to install special software. Worse, they could spend their e-cash in only a very few places.

Despite that sobering experience, a second generation of financial firms is now giving e-cash another go, online. Hardly a week passes without a start-up venture – usually American – announcing a new form of electronic money. And this time, the prospects look rather better.

There appears now to be genuine demand for an online alternative to credit cards, which the rapid growth of e-commerce is bound to fuel. Sometimes, consumers will wish to remain anonymous. Many, particularly outside America, have no access to plastic money. Some are too young. And auctions and other sorts of consumer-to-consumer e-commerce have created a need for online payment between individuals.

A survey carried out by Jupiter Communications

last year found that consumers are dissatisfied with the way they spend their money online (see). Jupiter predicts that the hegemony of credit cards online will wane – but not much. It forecasts a drop from 95% to 81% of the value of such transactions by 2003.

Merchants, for their part, might welcome digital cash – after all, credit-card costs take a hefty bite out of their revenue. That is a particular problem for the growing number of websites that sell cheap items – single songs, say. Most of the new financial firms working on e-cash are looking at "micropayments" – meaning purchases costing from a tenth of a cent to $10. One way to make such tiny sales worth a merchant's while is to store value in an online account and deduct small purchases. 1ClickCharge pioneered this approach. Two big computer firms, Compaq and IBM , have developed similar technology. Other firms, such as Qpass, make no initial charge, but accumulate payments and deduct the balance from a credit card. Trivnet and IPin are using Internet service providers to track customers' on-line spending and add it to their monthly bill.

Useful as these services may be, they are little more than an extension of existing payment systems. Another group of firms is trying to go further. Robert Levitan, chief executive and founder of a company called flooz.com, blames the failure of the first generation of e-cash on its lack of a compelling application. Flooz's answer is gift certificates. Consumers need them, says Mr Levitan, because they often lack time and gift ideas. And merchants like them, because consumers tend to spend them more readily than cash. In this system, present-givers, using a credit card, pay money into an account. They then e-mail it to the recipient, who can spend it at any of 68 merchant "partners". $5m-worth of flooz certificates are "in circulation".

Another company, Beenz.com, is taking a different approach. What Philip Letts, its chief executive, calls its "big gotcha" is that consumers can earn "beenz" simply by being online. About 50 websites use them to pay people for visiting, filling in online surveys or shopping. Beenz can be spent at other websites. The firm sells its currency to partner merchants at a rate of 100 to the dollar, of which half is its commission; so one beenz is worth half a cent. A similar scheme, run by Cybergold, even allows "cyberdollars" to be converted into real bucks.

A more significant source of competition may come from the offline world. The 38m members of American Airlines' frequent-flyer programme will from May 2000 be able not only to earn mileage points by purchasing goods and services on AOL , the world's largest online service. They will also be able to spend them there. To keep their mileage programmes attractive, other airlines may have to follow suit. This could unlock considerable buying power. Frequent Flyer Services, a consultancy, estimates that there are currently more than 3 trillion unused air-miles. Since airlines sell miles for between one and three cents, that lot will be worth somewhere between $30 billion and $90 billion.

Schemes such as Beenz and Cybergold, are, in essence, rewards programmes. David Birch, director of Consult Hyperion, a British e-cash consultancy, argues that, since consumers cannot pay each other with beenz or mileage points, they do not qualify as genuine digital money. One technology that does is PayPal, developed by Confinity. After opening an account on the company's website, people can e-mail dollars to others. Or users can download money to one Palm handheld computer and transfer it to another via infra-red signals.

Another firm, e-gold, also enables individuals to exchange money easily, but in a rather unusual way that creates a sort of gold standard for the Internet. Customers fund their online accounts by buying gold or other precious metals. They can then transfer units of those metals (measured in weight) on e-gold's website by entering a recipient's account number and a password. E-gold, which is rooted in libertarian thinking, has an ambitious vision of a "risk-free" financial system whose currency is fully backed by a physical commodity.

Other private currencies are in use on the on-line barter exchanges set up recently by such firms as BarterTrust, BigVine and LassoBucks. To make cashless exchanges of goods and services easier, they have had to create their own trading currencies. To establish trust in them some even have monetary governance structures. BigVine, for example, is trying to patent its "monetary policy".

Falling short

This new generation of e-cash firms appears to be getting more things right than its predecessor did. Confinity boasts 185,000 customers, Flooz.com about 450,000 and Beenz.com more than 720,000. Most of them are growing rapidly – partly because they usually pay new users $10 apiece.

But the schemes are far from the digital ideal. Most keep track of what users buy, and so fail to meet demands for anonymity and privacy. And many limit how their money can be spent. The products that offer the most anonymity and liquidity – especially if they can also be spent offline – have the best long-term prospects. Confinity's technology, for example, will soon be available for cell phones. Users will be able to beam money to vending machines – a service already on trial in Finland (albeit using different technology).

Even if e-cash version 2.0 fails, there will certainly be a version 3.0 – not least because technology is making it increasingly easy to come up with new schemes. Oakington, a British firm, has developed a standard software platform that other organisations can use to issue their own currency. The system boasts some subtleties. It allows for automatic payment of taxes and "time escrow", so that a transaction does not clear before goods are delivered.

Technology will also make it possible – and cheap – to turn financial assets such as mutual funds into money. There is no reason, argues Hyperion's Mr Birch, why consumers should not be able to pay their bills directly with units of a mutual fund, instead of having to go through a bank.

If the new e-cash proves hugely successful, will consumers start to prefer it to national currencies? That is unlikely. It will be a long time before consumers have the same trust in electronic bills issued, say, by Microsoft as in such proven brands as the dollar or the D-mark. A rational choice: companies go bankrupt, but the Fed has staying power.

Yet, even if their currencies are unlikely to be wholly replaced by digital creations, central banks cannot afford to ignore other threats posed by technology. It is, for example, making foreign-exchange transactions much cheaper. Services such as PayPal or e-gold might make it easier for residents of a country with a weak currency to shift their savings into a stronger one. The dollarisation of a country might one day become a mere matter of mouse clicks. Ultimately information technology could, in theory, lead to a pure exchange economy with real-time electronic transactions. And then central bankers' nightmares about their own obsolescence might finally come true.

This article appeared in The Economist *in February 2000*

Bubbles and scams

The are many instances of large numbers of people being persuaded to part with their money on the basis of what can be termed a "false prospectus". Here are two of the most notorious and one that, although it was a huge scandal at the time, is not nearly so well known.

Tulipmania

Tulips were introduced into Western Europe from Turkey in the 16th century. In the 17th century they gave rise to one of the most curious episodes in Holland's history. In the early 1600s single-colour tulips were being sold at relatively modest prices in Dutch markets but as new varieties were created, the fashion for tulips intensified and prices soared. By 1623 a particularly admired and rare variety, *Semper Augustus*, was selling for a thousand florins for a single bulb, more than six times the annual average wage. Ten years later the price had increased by more than fivefold, reaching a peak at the height of the tulip craze of some 10,000 florins, roughly the same as it cost to buy a fine canalside house in the centre of Amsterdam.

As the mania took hold more and more people sought to cash in on the boom – as growers, traders and then speculators as the tulip business developed from dealing in actual bulbs to dealing in what were in effect tulip futures – even going to the extent of selling their businesses or valuable possessions to do so.

It couldn't last, and it didn't. In 1637 the bulb bubble burst when it became clear that at the end of the long chain of those speculating in bulb futures there was no-one who actually wanted to buy the bulbs at such high prices. Within a period of a few months the market had crashed leaving thousands ruined.

The South Sea Bubble

In 1711 the South Sea Company was given a monopoly of all trade to the South Seas in return for assuming a portion of the national debt that

England had accumulated during the War of Spanish Succession, which had started in 1703 and was still continuing. It was anticipated that when the war ended, which it did in 1713, there would be rich trade pickings to be had among the Spanish colonies in South America. But the South Sea Company did little trading, preferring to accumulate money from investors attracted by its future prospects.

War between Spain and England broke out again in 1718 and the following year the South Sea Company made a proposal to assume the whole of England's national debt. Inducements were offered to influential people and the proposal was accepted. New shares were issued in the company and the stock price was talked up and up.

Speculation fever took hold; a large number of companies that were to trade in the "New World" or which had other supposedly promising futures were set up, many of which were plain and simple scams to separate investors from their money. Confidence in the market was dented and in an effort encouraged by the managers of the South Sea Company to restore it, the "Bubble Act" was passed in 1720 requiring all joint stock companies to have a royal charter. It did the trick: the South Sea Company's share price increased more than fivefold in four months to reach over £1,000. And then the bubble burst – or rather started to deflate. A gradual slide in the share price accelerated and within three months the company was worthless. Many were ruined and a committee set up in 1721 to investigate the affair discovered widespread corruption involving businessmen and politicians.

The Humbert scandal

This enormous but largely forgotten fraud nearly brought down the French Third Republic when it was still reeling from the Dreyfus Affair. Thérèse Humbert was the daughter of two illegitimate peasants from near Toulouse in France. Forty years later – despite plain looks – she was at the apex of Paris society, regularly entertaining the president, prime minister and former prime ministers and wearing fabulous diamonds and sapphires. She had another chateau outside Paris and spent 130,000 francs (some $400,000 at today's prices) on dresses.

How did she do it? There were three essential ingredients to this most elegant of scams. First, Thérèse was a brilliant storyteller. She was utterly persuasive in her tales and could dupe creditors, lawyers and bankers. Secondly, she was married to the son of the Minister of Justice, which both put her above criticism and gave her the support of one of the finest legal brains of his day. Third, there were the documents. Thérèse claimed to be the bastard daughter of an American billionaire called Robert Crawford. She had in her possession two "wills" dated September 1877. One left everything to her. The other left everything to his two "nephews". Another document was an agreement from the "nephews" to let Thérèse keep the fortune until the legal position was resolved. Last there were said to be bearer bonds worth 200 million francs (about a third of a billion dollars today). The breathtaking audaciousness of the scam was essential to its success.

Because of the legal dispute Thérèse claimed she could not use her inheritance. So she borrowed against it on a heroic scale. Huge sums came from bankers and industrialists (6 million francs from a distiller who was murdered when he became too clamorous for repayment) and life savings from shopkeepers, and small investors who put their money into a bank she created.

Inevitably, the creditors became increasingly restless and it finally came unstuck in 1902. Thousands were ruined. There were suicides and the government were nearly brought down. Therese and her family were arrested, tried and sentenced to hard labour. After her release from prison she disappeared completely.

PART 6

GOVERNMENTS
AND MONEY

Raising money

Government revenues are raised largely through taxes, social security contributions, fees or charges for services, and some miscellaneous sources such as interest on government loans. A few governments also conduct trading activities which generate income.

For the industrial countries as a group in the 1980s, personal income taxes, payroll taxes (largely social security) and taxes on spending each accounted for 25–30% of the total tax take. The remaining 16% came mainly from taxes on company profits and property.

One other source of income is receipts from the privatisation of activities previously undertaken by the public sector. In some countries, such as Britain, the receipts are classified as "negative expenditure". Either way, they have a once-off effect on public finances which is perhaps akin to selling the family silver and should not be mistaken for an underlying improvement.

In addition to financing government spending, taxes also have an important automatic stabilising influence. The government tax take increases and helps to moderate consumer demand when more people are earning and spending more at the top of the economic cycle. Similarly, the tax take declines during recession and to some extent helps to offset falling wage incomes.

Progressive or regressive

- **Progressive taxes** take a larger proportion of cash from the rich than from the poor, such as income tax where the marginal percentage rate of tax increases as income rises.
- **Proportional taxes** take the same percentage of everyone's income, wealth or expenditure, but the rich pay a larger amount in total.
- **Regressive taxes** take more from the poor. For example, a flat-rate tax of £200, such as Britain's controversial and short-lived poll tax,

takes a greater proportion of the income of a lower-paid worker than of a higher-paid worker.

Direct or indirect

Direct taxes. These are levied directly on people or companies. They include taxes on personal and corporate income, capital gains, capital transfers, inheritances and wealth; and royalties on mineral extraction.

Direct taxes are usually charged at percentage rates; frequently they are progressive. Payroll taxes tend to be regressive if considered separately from the associated social security benefits.

Social security payments are mostly financed by specific employers' and employees' contributions. Where these are passed through a separate social security budget, "headline" revenue figures are lower. On the other hand, Denmark's social security bill is mainly met from general taxation, which depresses the apparent level of social security revenues.

Indirect taxes. Levied on goods and services, these include:

- Value-added tax (VAT) charged on the value added at each stage of production; this amounts to a single tax on the final sale price.
- Sales and turnover taxes which may be levied on every transaction (for example, wheat, flour, bread).
- Customs duties on imports.
- Excise duties on home-produced goods, sometimes at penal rates to discourage activities such as smoking.

Indirect taxes tend to be regressive, as poorer people spend a bigger slice of their income. They are charged at either flat or percentage rates. Flat-rate duties do not rise with inflation and have to be "revalorised", usually in the annual budget, if the government is to retain its real tax-take.

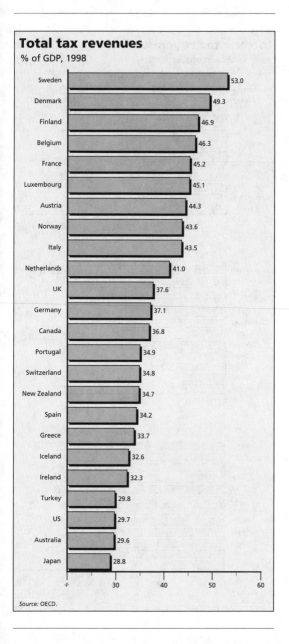

Total tax revenues
% of GDP, 1998

Country	%
Sweden	53.0
Denmark	49.3
Finland	46.9
Belgium	46.3
France	45.2
Luxembourg	45.1
Austria	44.3
Norway	43.6
Italy	43.5
Netherlands	41.0
UK	37.6
Germany	37.1
Canada	36.8
Portugal	34.9
Switzerland	34.8
New Zealand	34.7
Spain	34.2
Greece	33.7
Iceland	32.6
Ireland	32.3
Turkey	29.8
US	29.7
Australia	29.6
Japan	28.8

30   40   50   60

Source: OECD.

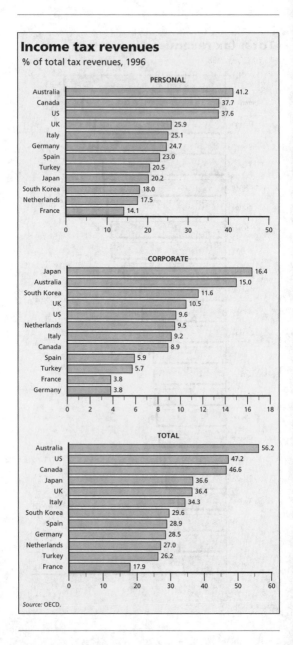

Income tax revenues

% of total tax revenues, 1996

PERSONAL

Australia	41.2
Canada	37.7
US	37.6
UK	25.9
Italy	25.1
Germany	24.7
Spain	23.0
Turkey	20.5
Japan	20.2
South Korea	18.0
Netherlands	17.5
France	14.1

CORPORATE

Japan	16.4
Australia	15.0
South Korea	11.6
UK	10.5
US	9.6
Netherlands	9.5
Italy	9.2
Canada	8.9
Spain	5.9
Turkey	5.7
France	3.8
Germany	3.8

TOTAL

Australia	56.2
US	47.2
Canada	46.6
Japan	36.6
UK	36.4
Italy	34.3
South Korea	29.6
Spain	28.9
Germany	28.5
Netherlands	27.0
Turkey	26.2
France	17.9

Source: OECD.

Tax revenues
% of GDP

| | Total | | by type, 1996 | | | | | |
	1990	1996	Income & profits	Social security	Payroll	Property	Goods & services	Other
US	26.9	28.5	13.5	7.0	–	3.1	4.9	–
Japan	25.4	28.4	10.4	10.4	–	3.2	4.4	0.1
Germany	38.2	38.1	10.8	15.5	–	1.1	10.6	0.0
France	41.7	45.7	8.2	19.7	1.0	2.3	12.5	2.0
UK	35.1	36.0	13.2	6.2	–	3.8	12.7	0.0
Italy	30.4	43.2	14.9	14.8	0.1	2.3	11.2	–
Mexico	16.2	16.3	4.1	2.5	–	–	9.3	0.3
Canada	32.0	36.8	17.4	6.0	–	3.8	9.1	0.4
Spain	23.9	33.7	9.8	12.1	–	1.9	9.8	0.1
South Korea	17.5	23.2	7.0	2.1	0.1	3.1	10.2	0.8
Turkey	17.9	25.4	6.7	4.0	–	0.5	9.7	4.6
Australia	28.4	31.1	17.5	–	2.1	2.8	8.7	–
Netherlands	45.2	43.3	11.7	17.1	–	1.9	12.4	0.2

Source: OECD.

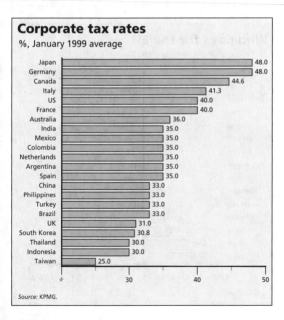

Corporate tax rates
%, January 1999 average

Japan	48.0
Germany	48.0
Canada	44.6
Italy	41.3
US	40.0
France	40.0
Australia	36.0
India	35.0
Mexico	35.0
Colombia	35.0
Netherlands	35.0
Argentina	35.0
Spain	35.0
China	33.0
Philippines	33.0
Turkey	33.0
Brazil	33.0
UK	31.0
South Korea	30.8
Thailand	30.0
Indonesia	30.0
Taiwan	25.0

Source: KPMG.

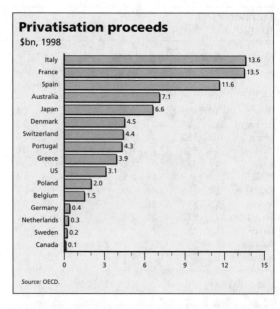

Privatisation proceeds
$bn, 1998

Italy	13.6
France	13.5
Spain	11.6
Australia	7.1
Japan	6.6
Denmark	4.5
Switzerland	4.4
Portugal	4.3
Greece	3.9
US	3.1
Poland	2.0
Belgium	1.5
Germany	0.4
Netherlands	0.3
Sweden	0.2
Canada	0.1

Source: OECD.

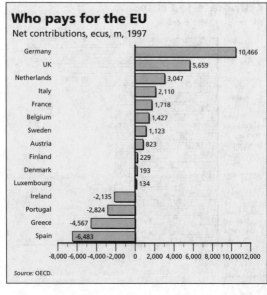

Who pays for the EU
Net contributions, ecus, m, 1997

Germany	10,466
UK	5,659
Netherlands	3,047
Italy	2,110
France	1,718
Belgium	1,427
Sweden	1,123
Austria	823
Finland	229
Denmark	193
Luxembourg	134
Ireland	-2,135
Portugal	-2,824
Greece	-4,567
Spain	-6,483

Source: OECD.

... and spending it

Government spending provides services including law and order, defence, education and health, roads, and so on. Such spending is an injection to the circular flow of income and has a considerable effect on aggregate demand. It is a stabilising influence to the extent that payments of welfare benefits increase when unemployment rises, which helps to maintain consumer spending.

Public spending may be classified in several different ways.

- **By level of government:** central and local authorities, state or provincial authorities for federations, social security funds and public corporations.
- **By department:** agriculture, defence, trade, and so on.
- **By function:** such as environmental services, which might be provided by more than one department.
- **By economic category:** current, capital, and so on.

Major categories of current spending include the following.

- Pay of public sector employees.
- Other current spending on goods and services.
- Subsidies such as public housing and agricultural support.
- Social security.
- Interest on the national debt.

Other current spending on goods and services exceed 20% of GDP in countries such as Sweden and Denmark where many services are supplied by the government rather than the private sector.

Capital spending is mainly fixed investment in infrastructure and dwellings. Note that some spending is arbitrarily classified as current spending even when there is a considerable capital outlay, such as in defence.

General government spending
% of GDP, 1996

	Total	Defence	Public order	Education	Health	Social security & welfare	Housing & community amenities
Australia	16.7	1.7	1.3	3.5	3.1	1.0	0.4
Austria	18.4	0.9	0.9	4.3	5.1	3.4	-0.1
Belgium	16.5	2.5	1.6	6.1	0.5	1.0	0.2
Denmark	25.2	1.8	1.0	5.6	5.0	6.7	0.2
France	19.8	3.1	0.9	5.2	3.4	1.5	1.4
Germany	19.9	1.4	1.6	3.7	6.6	3.0	0.3
Italy	16.3	1.7	1.7	4.2	3.4	0.7	0.5
Japan	9.7	0.9	n.a	3.2	0.4	0.7	0.7
Netherlands	14.0	2.7	n.a.	4.5	n.a.	0.7	n.a.
Spain	16.7	1.5	2.1	3.8	4.0	0.8	0.8
Sweden	26.2	2.4	1.4	5.1	4.6	5.7	0.5
UK	21.1	3.2	2.0	4.5	5.7	1.9	0.6
USA	15.7	n.a.	n.a.	n.a.	n.a.	n.a.	n.a.

Source: OECD.

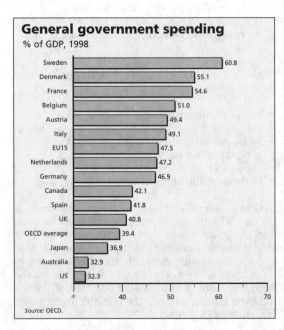

General government spending
% of GDP, 1998

Sweden	60.8
Denmark	55.1
France	54.6
Belgium	51.0
Austria	49.4
Italy	49.1
EU15	47.5
Netherlands	47.2
Germany	46.9
Canada	42.1
Spain	41.8
UK	40.8
OECD average	39.4
Japan	36.9
Australia	32.9
US	32.3

Source: OECD.

Debt

The public or national debt is the cumulative total of all government borrowing less repayments. It is financed mainly by citizens and may be seen as a transfer between generations. This contrasts with external (foreign) debt which has to be financed out of export earnings.

The national debt is often understated since governments carry various liabilities which do not show on their balance sheets. For example, public-sector pensions are usually unfunded, that is, paid out of current income rather than from a reserve created during the individual's working life as happens with private-sector pensions.

Economic theory provides few clues to the optimum ratio of public debt to GDP. Trends over time are often a better measure of a government's creditworthiness than the absolute level of debt. A country with an ever-rising debt ratio is clearly heading for trouble.

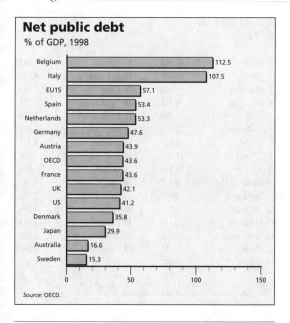

Net public debt
% of GDP, 1998

Belgium	112.5
Italy	107.5
EU15	57.1
Spain	53.4
Netherlands	53.3
Germany	47.6
Austria	43.9
OECD	43.6
France	43.6
UK	42.1
US	41.2
Denmark	35.8
Japan	29.9
Australia	16.6
Sweden	15.3

Source: OECD.

Highest foreign debt[a]
$m, 1998

1	Brazil	232,004	19	Egypt	31,964
2	Russia	183,601	20	Algeria	30,665
3	Mexico	159,959	21	Nigeria	30,315
4	China	154,599	22	Hungary	28,580
5	Indonesia	147,475	23	Czech Republic	25,301
6	Argentina	144,050	24	South Africa	24,711
7	South Korea	139,097	25	Syria	22,435
8	Turkey	102,074	26	Vietnam	22,359
9	India	98,232	27	Morocco	20,687
10	Thailand	86,172	28	Sudan	16,843
11	Philippines	47,817	29	Bangladesh	16,376
12	Poland	47,708	30	Ecuador	15,140
13	Malaysia	44,773	31	Côte d'Ivoire	14,852
14	Venezuela	37,003	32	Iran	14,391
15	Chile	36,302	33	Serbia & Mont	13,742
16	Colombia	33,263	34	Congo	12,929
17	Peru	32,397	35	Ukraine	12,718
18	Pakistan	32,229	36	Angola	12,173

Highest debt service[b]
$m, 1998

1	Brazil	46,365	17	Poland	4,284
2	Mexico	25,663	18	Colombia	4,217
3	Argentina	19,078	19	Chile	4,039
4	Indonesia	17,461	20	South Africa	3,324
5	China	16,784	21	Morocco	2,794
6	South Korea	14,645	22	Iran	2,667
7	Thailand	11,575	23	Pakistan	2,436
8	Turkey	11,507	24	Romania	2,095
9	India	11,343	25	Slovakia	1,954
10	Russia	9,129	26	Peru	1,860
11	Hungary	6,947	27	Ukraine	1,759
12	Malaysia	5,615	28	Egypt	1,586
13	Venezuela	5,175	29	Ecuador	1,529
14	Czech Republic	4,983	30	Angola	1,308
15	Philippines	4,751	31	Côte d'Ivoire	1,285
16	Algeria	4,587		Tunisia	1,285

a Foreign debt is debt owed to non-residents and repayable in foreign currency; the figures shown include liabilities of government, public and private sectors. Developed countries have been excluded.

Highest foreign debt burden
Foreign debt as % of GDP, 1998

1	Guinea-Bissau	503.6	19	Gambia, The	116.7
2	Congo	306.9	20	Jordan	116.0
3	Angola	297.1	21	Yemen	104.8
4	Mauritania	272.5	22	Guinea	102.0
5	Mozambique	223.0	23	Togo	97.4
6	Zambia	217.4	24	Honduras	96.9
7	Congo	208.2	25	Tanzania	94.3
8	Laos	199.1	26	Macedonia	92.6
9	Sierra Leone	197.7	27	Ghana	91.8
10	Sudan	182.7	28	Gabon	90.7
11	Indonesia	172.5	29	Central African Rep	88.8
12	Ethiopia	160.4	30	Turkmenistan	87.7
13	Côte d'Ivoire	145.4	31	Senegal	83.1
14	Malawi	137.5	32	Bulgaria	83.0
15	Mali	120.4	33	Ecuador	82.5
16	Madagascar	119.5	34	Vietnam	82.3
17	Cameroon	119.4	35	Niger	82.1
18	Burundi	119.1	36	Zimbabwe	79.8

Highest debt service ratios[b]
%, 1998

1	Brazil	73.0	17	Guinea-Bissau	25.6
2	Argentina	58.2	18	Ecuador	25.2
3	Burundi	49.1	19	Uganda	23.6
4	Algeria	46.0	20	Romania	23.5
5	Turkmenistan	42.0		Uruguay	23.5
6	Zimbabwe	38.2	22	Senegal	23.2
7	Angola	34.4	23	Chile	22.3
8	Indonesia	32.6	24	Bulgaria	22.1
9	Colombia	29.7	25	Cameroon	21.7
10	Bolivia	29.0	26	Nicaragua	21.1
11	Ghana	27.9	27	Central African Rep	20.9
12	Mauritania	27.6		Pakistan	20.9
13	Venezuela	27.4	29	Tanzania	20.8
14	Hungary	27.2	30	Iran	20.2
15	Peru	27.1	31	Mexico	20.0
16	Côte d'Ivoire	26.1	32	Morocco	19.7

b Debt service is the sum of interest and principal repayments (amortization)
due on outstanding foreign debt. The debt service ratio is debt service
expressed as a percentage of the country's exports of goods and services.

Aid

Largest bilateral and multilateral donors
$m, 1998

1	Japan	10,640	13	Australia	960
2	United States	8,786	14	Switzerland	898
3	France	5,742	15	Belgium	883
4	Germany	5,581	16	Austria	456
5	United Kingdom	3,864	17	Finland	396
6	Netherlands	3,042	18	Saudi Arabia	288
7	Italy	2,278	19	Kuwait	278
8	Denmark	1,704	20	Portugal	259
9	Canada	1,691	21	Ireland	199
10	Sweden	1,573	22	South Korea	183
11	Spain	1,376	23	Greece	179
12	Norway	1,321	24	New Zealand	130

Largest recipients of bilateral and multilateral aid
$m, 1998

1	China	2,359	24	Madagascar	494
2	Egypt	1,915	25	Sri Lanka	490
3	India	1,595	26	Kenya	474
4	Indonesia	1,258	27	Uganda	471
5	Bangladesh	1,251	28	Malawi	434
6	Vietnam	1,163	29	Cameroon	424
7	Israel	1,066	30	Jordan	408
8	Pakistan	1,050	31	Haiti	407
9	Mozambique	1,039	32	Nepal	404
10	Tanzania	998	33	Burkina Faso	397
11	Bosnia	876	34	Algeria	389
12	Côte d'Ivoire	798	35	Papua New Guinea	361
13	Ghana	701	36	Guinea	359
14	Thailand	690	37	Rwanda	350
15	Ethiopia	648	38	Mali	349
16	Bolivia	628		Zambia	349
17	Philippines	607	40	Cambodia	337
18	West Bank and Gaza	598	41	Angola	335
19	Nicaragua	562	42	Brazil	329
20	Morocco	528	43	Honduras	318
21	South Africa	512		Jamaica	318
22	Senegal	502	45	Yemen	310
23	Peru	501	46	Niger	291

Largest bilateral and multilateral donors
% of GDP, 1998

1	Denmark	0.99		New Zealand	0.27
2	Norway	0.91		United Kingdom	0.27
3	Netherlands	0.80	15	Germany	0.26
4	Sweden	0.72	16	Spain	0.24
5	France	0.40		Portugal	0.24
6	Belgium	0.35	18	Austria	0.22
7	Finland	0.32	19	Italy	0.20
	Switzerland	0.32		Saudi Arabia	0.20
9	Ireland	0.30	21	Greece	0.14
10	Canada	0.29	22	Kuwait	0.10
11	Japan	0.28		United States	0.10
12	Australia	0.27	24	South Korea	0.04

Largest recipients of bilateral and multilateral aid
$ per head, 1998

1	Netherlands Antilles	606	26	Honduras	52
2	West Bank and Gaza	577	27	Haiti	51
3	Israel	178	28	Guinea	49
4	Bosnia	238	29	Kirgizstan	47
5	Suriname	143	30	Macedonia	46
6	Jamaica	125	31	Fiji	45
7	Nicaragua	117	32	Eritrea	44
8	Namibia	108	33	Malawi	42
9	Guinea-Bissau	83	34	Zambia	40
10	Bolivia	79	35	Armenia	39
	Mongolia	79		Gabon	39
12	Albania	78	37	Ghana	37
	Papua New Guinea	78	38	Benin	36
14	Lebanon	74	39	Burkina Faso	35
15	Bahrain	69		Mauritius	35
16	Botswana	68	41	Central African Rep	34
	Mauritania	68	42	Madagascar	33
18	Jordan	65		Mali	33
19	Barbados	60	44	Georgia	32
20	Malta	57		Lesotho	32
21	Côte d'Ivoire	56	46	Cambodia	31
	Senegal	56		Gambia, The	31
23	Mozambique	55		Tanzania	31
24	Laos	54	49	Cameroon	30
25	Rwanda	53	50	Egypt	29

PART 7

PEOPLE AND MONEY

PART 3

PEOPLE AND MONEY

Income and wealth

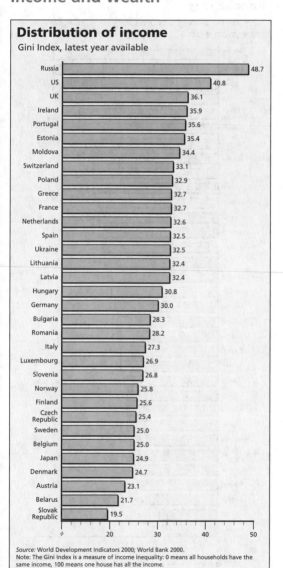

Distribution of income

Gini Index, latest year available

Russia	48.7
US	40.8
UK	36.1
Ireland	35.9
Portugal	35.6
Estonia	35.4
Moldova	34.4
Switzerland	33.1
Poland	32.9
Greece	32.7
France	32.7
Netherlands	32.6
Spain	32.5
Ukraine	32.5
Lithuania	32.4
Latvia	32.4
Hungary	30.8
Germany	30.0
Bulgaria	28.3
Romania	28.2
Italy	27.3
Luxembourg	26.9
Slovenia	26.8
Norway	25.8
Finland	25.6
Czech Republic	25.4
Sweden	25.0
Belgium	25.0
Japan	24.9
Denmark	24.7
Austria	23.1
Belarus	21.7
Slovak Republic	19.5

Source: World Development Indicators 2000; World Bank 2000.
Note: The Gini Index is a measure of income inequality: 0 means all households have the same income, 100 means one house has all the income.

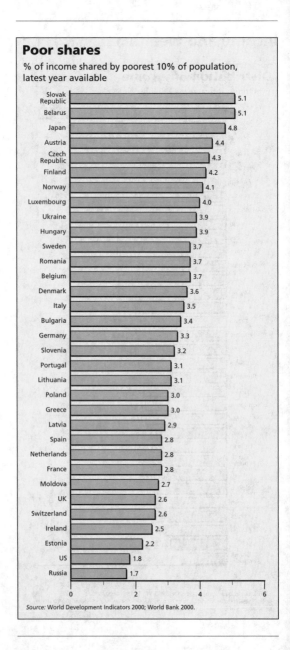

Poor shares

% of income shared by poorest 10% of population, latest year available

Slovak Republic	5.1
Belarus	5.1
Japan	4.8
Austria	4.4
Czech Republic	4.3
Finland	4.2
Norway	4.1
Luxembourg	4.0
Ukraine	3.9
Hungary	3.9
Sweden	3.7
Romania	3.7
Belgium	3.7
Denmark	3.6
Italy	3.5
Bulgaria	3.4
Germany	3.3
Slovenia	3.2
Portugal	3.1
Lithuania	3.1
Poland	3.0
Greece	3.0
Latvia	2.9
Spain	2.8
Netherlands	2.8
France	2.8
Moldova	2.7
UK	2.6
Switzerland	2.6
Ireland	2.5
Estonia	2.2
US	1.8
Russia	1.7

Source: World Development Indicators 2000; World Bank 2000.

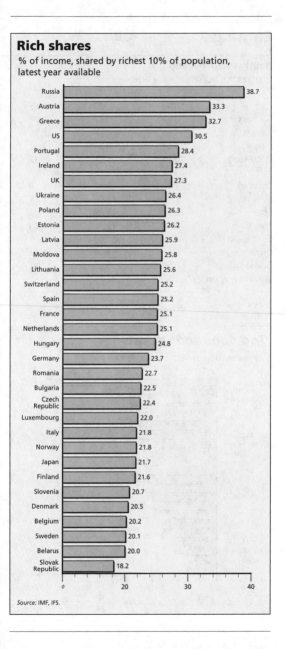

Rich shares

% of income, shared by richest 10% of population, latest year available

Russia	38.7
Austria	33.3
Greece	32.7
US	30.5
Portugal	28.4
Ireland	27.4
UK	27.3
Ukraine	26.4
Poland	26.3
Estonia	26.2
Latvia	25.9
Moldova	25.8
Lithuania	25.6
Switzerland	25.2
Spain	25.2
France	25.1
Netherlands	25.1
Hungary	24.8
Germany	23.7
Romania	22.7
Bulgaria	22.5
Czech Republic	22.4
Luxembourg	22.0
Italy	21.8
Norway	21.8
Japan	21.7
Finland	21.6
Slovenia	20.7
Denmark	20.5
Belgium	20.2
Sweden	20.1
Belarus	20.0
Slovak Republic	18.2

Source: IMF, IFS.

Earnings

Hourly compensation
$, production workers in manufacturing

	1975	1980	1985
Australia	5.62	8.47	8.20
Canada	5.96	8.67	10.95
France	4.52	8.94	7.52
Hong Kong	0.76	1.51	1.73
Italy	4.67	8.15	7.63
Japan	3.00	5.52	6.34
Netherlands	6.58	12.06	8.75
Spain	2.53	5.89	4.66
Sweden	7.18	12.51	9.66
Switzerland	6.09	11.09	9.66
United Kingdom	3.37	7.56	6.27
United States	6.36	9.87	13.01
Western Germany	6.31	12.25	9.53

Source: US Bureau of Labour Statistics.

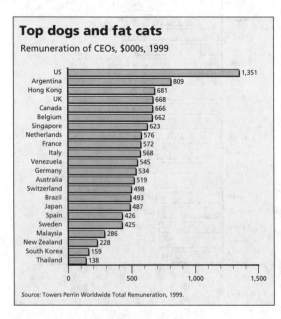

Top dogs and fat cats

Remuneration of CEOs, $000s, 1999

Source: Towers Perrin Worldwide Total Remuneration, 1999.

1990	1995	1998
13.07	15.27	14.90
15.95	16.10	15.60
15.49	20.01	18.20
3.20	4.82	5.40
17.45	16.22	17.10
12.80	23.82	18.00
18.06	24.02	20.50
11.38	12.88	12.10
20.93	21.44	22.00
20.86	29.30	24.30
12.70	13.67	16.40
14.91	17.19	18.50
21.88	31.76	27.90

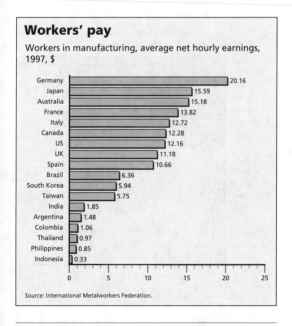

Workers' pay

Workers in manufacturing, average net hourly earnings, 1997, $

Country	Earnings
Germany	20.16
Japan	15.59
Australia	15.18
France	13.82
Italy	12.72
Canada	12.28
US	12.16
UK	11.18
Spain	10.66
Brazil	6.36
South Korea	5.94
Taiwan	5.75
India	1.85
Argentina	1.48
Colombia	1.06
Thailand	0.97
Philippines	0.85
Indonesia	0.33

Source: International Metalworkers Federation.

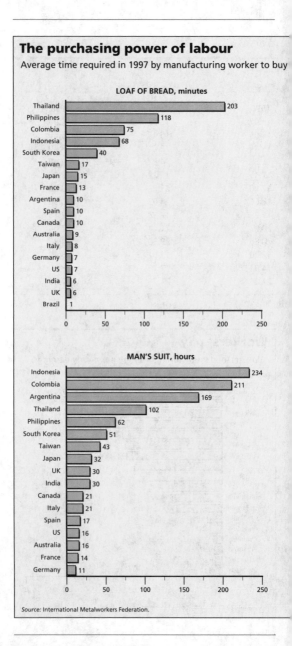

The purchasing power of labour

Average time required in 1997 by manufacturing worker to buy

LOAF OF BREAD, minutes

Thailand	203
Philippines	118
Colombia	75
Indonesia	68
South Korea	40
Taiwan	17
Japan	15
France	13
Argentina	10
Spain	10
Canada	10
Australia	9
Italy	8
Germany	7
US	7
India	6
UK	6
Brazil	1

MAN'S SUIT, hours

Indonesia	234
Colombia	211
Argentina	169
Thailand	102
Philippines	62
South Korea	51
Taiwan	43
Japan	32
UK	30
India	30
Canada	21
Italy	21
Spain	17
US	16
Australia	16
France	14
Germany	11

Source: International Metalworkers Federation.

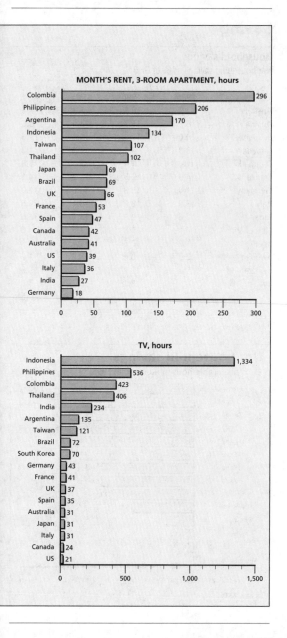

MONTH'S RENT, 3-ROOM APARTMENT, hours

Colombia	296
Philippines	206
Argentina	170
Indonesia	134
Taiwan	107
Thailand	102
Japan	69
Brazil	69
UK	66
France	53
Spain	47
Canada	42
Australia	41
US	39
Italy	36
India	27
Germany	18

TV, hours

Indonesia	1,334
Philippines	536
Colombia	423
Thailand	406
India	234
Argentina	135
Taiwan	121
Brazil	72
South Korea	70
Germany	43
France	41
UK	37
Spain	35
Australia	31
Japan	31
Italy	31
Canada	24
US	21

Saving

Household savings
Net household savings as % of GDP

	1985	1990	1995	1998
Australia	7.3	6.8	1.3	2.5
Austria	8.3	13.7	13.4	8.6
Belgium	14.0	17.1	19.3	11.6
Canada	13.3	9.7	7.4	1.2
Denmark	n.a.	11.4	5.4	5.8
France	14.0	12.5	14.3	14.1
Germany	11.4	13.8	11.6	11.0
Italy	18.9	18.2	13.1	11.5
Japan	15.6	12.1	13.4	13.6
Netherlands	0.1	5.8	1.8	-0.6
Spain	11.2	10.5	11.7	10.5
Sweden	2.3	-0.6	8.2	1.2
Switzerland	5.7	12.2	9.9	9.0
UK	10.7	8.1	10.2	7.8
US	7.1	5.2	4.7	0.5

Source: OECD.

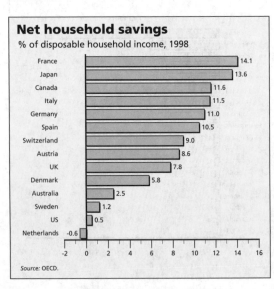

Net household savings
% of disposable household income, 1998

France	14.1
Japan	13.6
Canada	11.6
Italy	11.5
Germany	11.0
Spain	10.5
Switzerland	9.0
Austria	8.6
UK	7.8
Denmark	5.8
Australia	2.5
Sweden	1.2
US	0.5
Netherlands	-0.6

Source: OECD.

National savings
Gross national savings as % of GDP

	1985	1990	1995	1997
Australia	18.9	17.3	17.6	18.4
Austria	23.2	26.3	22.4	23.0
Belgium	15.0	21.0	22.5	22.4
Canada	19.6	16.4	17.8	18.4
Denmark	14.9	17.8	20.4	20.9
France	18.9	21.5	19.8	20.0
Germany	22.0	24.9	20.6	20.7
Italy	21.6	19.6	20.6	20.4
Japan	31.7	34.6	30.8	31.1
Netherlands	24.3	26.0	24.7	27.1
Spain	20.6	21.7	21.3	21.0
Sweden	17.5	17.7	16.7	16.1
Switzerland	29.8	33.1	28.5	29.0
UK	17.6	14.3	14.3	14.9
US	17.6	15.6	16.2	17.4
EU15	20.1	21.0	19.6	19.9
OECD	21.1	21.0	20.4	21.1

Source: OECD.

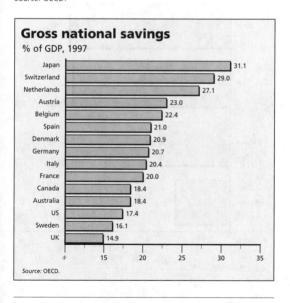

Gross national savings
% of GDP, 1997

Japan	31.1
Switzerland	29.0
Netherlands	27.1
Austria	23.0
Belgium	22.4
Spain	21.0
Denmark	20.9
Germany	20.7
Italy	20.4
France	20.0
Canada	18.4
Australia	18.4
US	17.4
Sweden	16.1
UK	14.9

Source: OECD.

Investing

Household equity holdings
% of net wealth

	1980–84	1985–89	1990–94	1995	1996	1997
United States	10.6	11	15.1	19.5	20.9	24.4
Japan	4.5	7.6	5.8	5.4	4.9	3.7
France	1.3	3.1	2.9	2.6	2.9	3.2
Italy	0.8	2.1	3.6	3.8	3.6	4.7
Britain	5.5	6.3	9.4	11.3	11.3	12.4
Canada	13.7	13.9	14.2	15.6	16.5	18.3

Source: IMF.

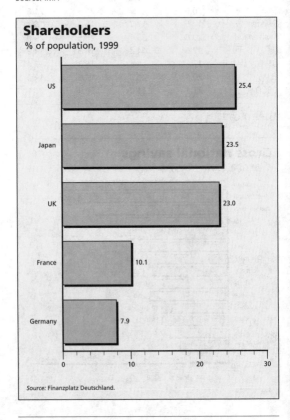

Shareholders
% of population, 1999

US	25.4
Japan	23.5
UK	23.0
France	10.1
Germany	7.9

Source: Finanzplatz Deutschland.

Home truths

Residential property prices
1994=100

	1990	1995	1998
Austria	81	103	108
Belgium	76	105	114
Britain	105	100	126
Denmark	93	100	124
Finland	145	97	132
France	90	95	101
Germany	74	98	101
Ireland	90	98	171
Italy	86	102	98
Japan	123	98	92
Netherlands	76	105	138
Spain	88	104	112
Sweden	111	101	119
United States	88	102	120

Source: European Central Bank

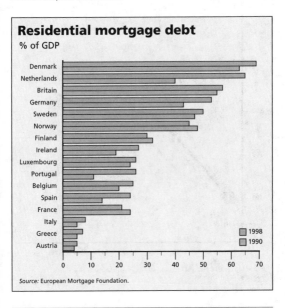

Residential mortgage debt
% of GDP

Denmark, Netherlands, Britain, Germany, Sweden, Norway, Finland, Ireland, Luxembourg, Portugal, Belgium, Spain, France, Italy, Greece, Austria

☐ 1998
☐ 1990

Source: European Mortgage Foundation.

Consumer spending

Consumer spending trends
Volume indices, 1960 = 100

	France	Germany	Italy	Japan	UK	US
1960	100.0	100.0	100.0	100.0	100.0	100.0
1970	168.5	164.6	186.6	237.3	126.4	150.7
1980	232.1	228.3	282.2	375.1	157.6	204.4
1990	291.5	283.3	371.7	540.5	221.7	277.0
1995	307.6	317.3	382.5	595.1	232.4	310.5
1996	311.6	319.8	386.0	612.4	240.7	320.8
1997	312.2	323.8	395.9	618.9	251.4	330.5
1998	323.3	329.7	403.2	612.4	258.2	349.0
1999	...	...	...	...	...	367.4

Source: Source:OECD National Accounts, Main Aggregates 1960–1997 Vol.1; Quarterly National Accounts.

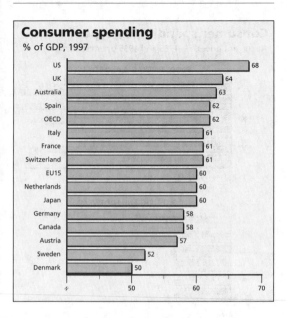

Consumer spending
% of GDP, 1997

US	68
UK	64
Australia	63
Spain	62
OECD	62
Italy	61
France	61
Switzerland	61
EU15	60
Netherlands	60
Japan	60
Germany	58
Canada	58
Austria	57
Sweden	52
Denmark	50

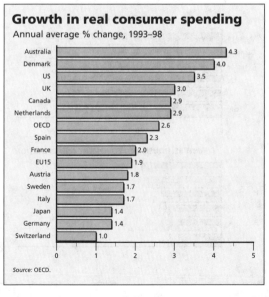

Growth in real consumer spending
Annual average % change, 1993–98

Australia	4.3
Denmark	4.0
US	3.5
UK	3.0
Canada	2.9
Netherlands	2.9
OECD	2.6
Spain	2.3
France	2.0
EU15	1.9
Austria	1.8
Sweden	1.7
Italy	1.7
Japan	1.4
Germany	1.4
Switzerland	1.0

Source: OECD.

Consumer spending by type

At current prices, %, 1985 and 1995 or latest year

FOOD, BEVERAGES AND TOBACCO

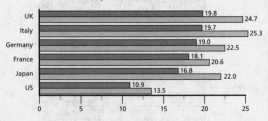

	1985	1995
UK	19.8	24.7
Italy	19.7	25.3
Germany	19.0	22.5
France	18.1	20.6
Japan	16.8	22.0
US	10.9	13.5

CLOTHING AND FOOTWEAR

	1985	1995
Italy	9.3	10.3
Germany	7.3	8.2
UK	5.8	6.9
US	5.7	6.2
France	5.4	7.0
Japan	5.1	6.6

RENT, FUEL AND POWER

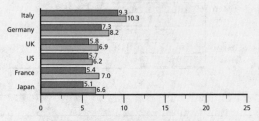

	1985	1995
Japan	22.2	18.6
Germany	22.0	21.8
France	21.7	19.0
UK	19.1	20.0
US	18.6	19.3
Italy	17.8	15.0

FURNITURE, HOUSEHOLD EQUIPMENT AND OPERATION

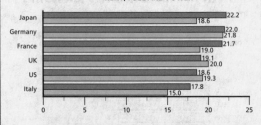

	1985	1995
Italy	9.3	9.1
Germany	8.9	8.4
France	7.3	8.3
UK	6.4	6.5
US	5.5	6.1
Japan	5.2	6.1

Source: UN Statistical Yearbooks.

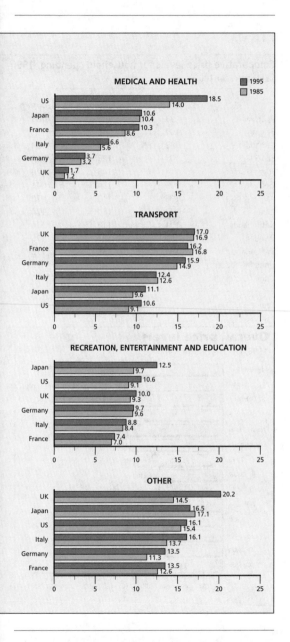

MEDICAL AND HEALTH

■ 1995
□ 1985

US: 18.5 / 14.0
Japan: 10.6 / 10.4
France: 10.3 / 8.6
Italy: 6.6 / 5.6
Germany: 3.7 / 3.2
UK: 1.7 / 1.2

TRANSPORT

UK: 17.0 / 16.9
France: 16.2 / 16.8
Germany: 15.9 / 14.9
Italy: 12.4 / 12.6
Japan: 11.1 / 9.6
US: 10.6 / 9.1

RECREATION, ENTERTAINMENT AND EDUCATION

Japan: 12.5 / 9.7
US: 10.6 / 9.1
UK: 10.0 / 9.3
Germany: 9.7 / 9.6
Italy: 8.8 / 8.4
France: 7.4 / 7.0

OTHER

UK: 20.2 / 14.5
Japan: 16.5 / 17.1
US: 16.1 / 15.4
Italy: 16.1 / 13.7
Germany: 13.5 / 11.3
France: 13.5 / 12.6

Prices

Comparative price levels for household spending, 1996
OECD average=100

	Food	*Clothing*	*Housing*
Australia	93	104	103
Belgium	109	142	113
Canada	83	100	84
EU15	107	123	104
France	114	145	129
Germany	109	134	141
Italy	106	113	70
Japan	187	150	174
Netherlands	101	118	124
Sweden	139	137	176
Switzerland	142	136	176
United Kingdom	105	97	80
United States	80	73	90

Source: OECD.

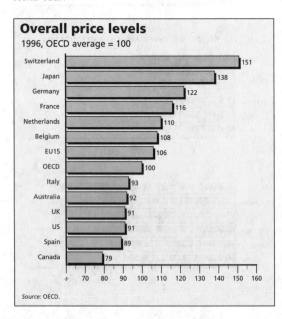

Overall price levels

1996, OECD average = 100

Switzerland	151
Japan	138
Germany	122
France	116
Netherlands	110
Belgium	108
EU15	106
OECD	100
Italy	93
Australia	92
UK	91
US	91
Spain	89
Canada	79

Source: OECD.

Health care	Transport & communication	Education
78	90	94
93	118	119
63	118	119
97	119	109
93	126	126
111	124	112
79	104	109
87	117	135
91	128	104
136	143	142
149	146	141
73	113	92
115	86	88

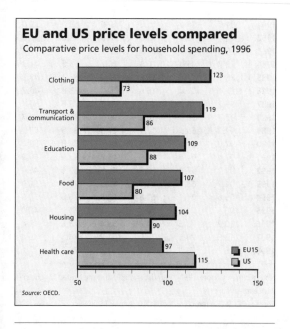

EU and US price levels compared

Comparative price levels for household spending, 1996

Clothing: EU15 123, US 73
Transport & communication: EU15 119, US 86
Education: EU15 109, US 88
Food: EU15 107, US 80
Housing: EU15 104, US 90
Health care: EU15 97, US 115

■ EU15
□ US

Source: OECD.

Consumer borrowing

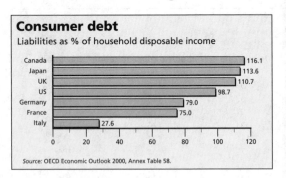

Consumer debt

Liabilities as % of household disposable income

Canada	116.1
Japan	113.6
UK	110.7
US	98.7
Germany	79.0
France	75.0
Italy	27.6

Source: OECD Economic Outlook 2000, Annex Table 58.

Liabilities
% of household disposable income

	Canada	of which mortgages	Germany	of which building loans	France	of which medium and long-term credit
1981	81.0	50.0	15.0	10.0	59.0	39.0
1982	74.0	45.0	15.0	10.0	58.0	39.0
1983	75.2	46.8	15.9	10.1	57.9	39.4
1984	72.7	45.4	16.1	10.1	63.5	41.3
1985	75.9	47.4	16.5	10.4	63.3	42.9
1986	82.1	51.4	16.6	10.7	68.8	46.7
1987	89.2	55.7	16.3	10.8	78.6	50.4
1988	92.3	58.0	16.2	10.9	86.4	52.7
1989	94.3	60.0	17.1	11.6	88.5	52.1
1990	97.0	61.7	66.7	51.1	88.8	52.1
1991	97.4	64.0	60.9	45.7	83.9	50.9
1992	99.7	66.9	60.8	45.4	82.1	48.4
1993	101.7	68.5	63.7	48.3	77.4	51.9
1994	105.6	71.1	67.8	52.3	76.0	50.6
1995	106.6	71.5	70.7	55.2	71.9	48.8
1996	110.2	73.6	74.0	58.4	73.8	49.4
1997	112.9	74.5	77.0	61.3	74.3	49.4
1998	116.1	75.5	79.0	63.3	75.0	...

Note: Germany (from 1990), Italy (from 1989) and the United Kingdom (from
with earlier years.
Source: OECD Economic Outlook 2000, Annex Table 58.

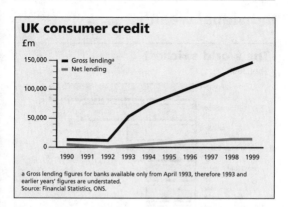

UK consumer credit

£m

- Gross lending[a]
- Net lending

150,000 —
100,000 —
50,000 —
0 —

1990 1991 1992 1993 1994 1995 1996 1997 1998 1999

a Gross lending figures for banks available only from April 1993, therefore 1993 and
earlier years' figures are understated.
Source: Financial Statistics, ONS.

Italy	of which medium and long-term credit	Japan	of which mortgages	UK	of which mortgages	US	of which mortgages
8.0	6.0	79.0	32.0	62.0	35.0	74.0	48.0
8.0	5.0	82.0	34.0	68.0	40.0	72.0	16.0
7.6	5.2	84.6	34.8	74.3	46.6	73.5	16.6
8.6	6.2	87.5	35.3	80.4	48.4	74.0	46.8
9.2	6.5	88.8	35.6	85.8	52.3	80.1	49.5
10.0	6.8	91.6	37.1	100.0	63.7	79.3	50.2
10.6	7.6	100.9	40.1	103.7	91.8	81.9	53.8
11.7	8.5	107.5	42.7	112.3	100.7	82.9	55.4
28.3	13.0	111.5	45.8	116.5	105.0	84.6	57.1
29.1	13.7	116.5	47.8	117.1	106.0	85.7	59.2
29.8	14.3	115.1	48.0	115.0	103.7	86.5	60.7
30.6	14.4	110.6	48.7	110.2	99.6	85.1	60.2
31.8	14.9	110.0	50.4	107.1	97.0	86.9	60.8
31.9	15.2	110.5	52.1	108.1	98.5	89.3	61.4
32.3	15.7	111.7	53.8	107.3	97.4	91.9	61.7
32.8	15.9	109.1	53.9	106.2	96.7	93.9	62.7
25.9	17.9	107.3	55.3	106.5	96.9	95.3	63.5
27.6	19.5	113.6	50.2	110.7	100.7	98.7	66.5

introduced a new methodology and figures are therefore not comparable

Individual wealth

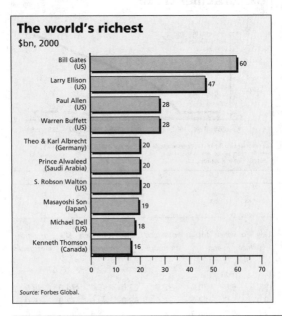

The world's richest
$bn, 2000

Bill Gates (US)	60
Larry Ellison (US)	47
Paul Allen (US)	28
Warren Buffett (US)	28
Theo & Karl Albrecht (Germany)	20
Prince Alwaleed (Saudi Arabia)	20
S. Robson Walton (US)	20
Masayoshi Son (Japan)	19
Michael Dell (US)	18
Kenneth Thomson (Canada)	16

Source: Forbes Global.

Family fortunes

Name	Country	Estimated net worth, $bn
Mulliez	France	11.0
Haniel	Germany	9.5
Seydoux/Schlumberger	France	8.6
Porsche/Piëch	Austria	5.8
Boehringer family	Germany	5.9
Defforey	France	5.1
Henkel family	Germany	4.5
Brenninkmeyer	Netherlands	4.5
Bin Mahfouz	Saudi Arabia	4.0
Wonowidjojo	Indonesia	2.6
Fleming	UK	2.3

Source: Forbes Global.

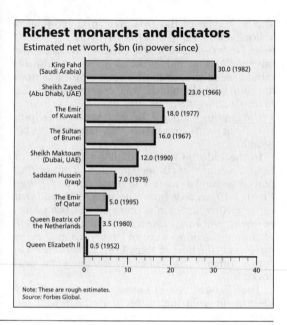

Richest monarchs and dictators

Estimated net worth, $bn (in power since)

King Fahd (Saudi Arabia)	30.0 (1982)
Sheikh Zayed (Abu Dhabi, UAE)	23.0 (1966)
The Emir of Kuwait	18.0 (1977)
The Sultan of Brunei	16.0 (1967)
Sheikh Maktoum (Dubai, UAE)	12.0 (1990)
Saddam Hussein (Iraq)	7.0 (1979)
The Emir of Qatar	5.0 (1995)
Queen Beatrix of the Netherlands	3.5 (1980)
Queen Elizabeth II	0.5 (1952)

Note: These are rough estimates.
Source: Forbes Global.

Source of wealth	*No. of people who share the fortune*
Retailing: Auchan	350, led by Gerard Mulliez
Metro stores, diversified holdings	930
Oilfield services: Schlumberger	at least 20
Porsche Holding, Porsche AG	about 50
Pharmaceuticals: Boehringer Ingelheim	at least 12
Retailing: Carrefour	60
Consumer goods: Henkel KGaA	80
Clothes retailing: American Retail Group; C&A	at least 150
Banking, farming	at least 13
Cigarettes: Gudang Garam	at least 8
Sale of Robert Fleming Holding to Chase Manhattan	about 20

The richest in ancient times

The archetype of the rich man in Greco-Roman antiquity was King Croesus of Lydia, in whose reign (c. 560–546BC) it was believed coinage was invented. Lydia and its kings grew wealthy on tributes from their subject Greek cities and from the alluvial gold which was collected from the River Pactolus. Croesus was extremely generous to the famous shrine of the god Apollo at Delphi. His dedications preserved the memory of his wealth.

In the Judaeo-Christian tradition the wealth of King Solomon of Israel (mid-10th century BC) played a similar role. The *First Book of Kings*, Chapter 10, records how "the weight of gold that came to King Solomon in one year was 666 talents of gold … All King Solomon's drinking cups were of pure gold, none were of silver … Once every three years the fleet of ships from Tarshish used to come bringing gold, silver, ivory, apes and peacocks."

The Persian kings were also proverbially wealthy in gold and silver compared with the poor Greeks. When Alexander the Great (reigned 336–323BC) conquered the Persian Empire, he took 180,000 talents (about 10.44m lb or 5.13m kg) of gold and silver from the royal treasuries.

In the Roman world there were a number of famously rich men. In the Republican period, the powerful politician Marcus Licinius Crassus (died 53BC) earned a huge fortune from buying up property in Rome cheaply in the wake of a wave of confiscations. He said that he would call no one wealthy unless they could support a whole legion (about 5,000 soldiers) from their own assets. In 62BC he was rich enough to be able to pay off Julius Caesar's debts, which were rumoured to amount to 25m denarii (for comparison, a year's pay for a solder at that time was 112.5 denarii; it was doubled in 46BC).

In Imperial Rome the richest man by far was the emperor. His personal wealth consisted of a massive network of estates and, importantly, precious metal mines throughout the empire. The first emperor, Augustus (reigned 31BC–14AD), took control not only of political power but also of the empire's wealth. In an autobiographical inscription, he recorded how during his reign he had donated to the public purse the colossal sum of 600m denarii. The reality was that the emperor's personal fortune was effectively indistinguishable from the official treasury, and was often in a much better state of financial health.

In the late Roman period there was an increasing gap between the super-rich, with estates throughout the empire, and the humble poor. One of the wealthiest was Symmachus, a brilliant orator and opponent of Christianity, who in 401AD paid out 2,000 Roman pounds of gold for his son's praetorian games (1 Roman pound = 325g). This was equivalent to 144,000 solidi, the coin in which gold circulated at the time. By contrast, the Hoxne hoard of coins from the same period (from Suffolk, England), the largest late Roman precious metal hoard yet found, was worth only about 2,000 solidi. Annual senatorial incomes ranged from 4,000 pounds of gold for the really wealthy to 1,500 pounds of gold for those of moderate fortune.

PART 8

MISCELLAMONEY

Bank robberies

It is estimated that in 1998 more than $77 billion was stolen from banks in the United States; this was some $26 billion less than in 1997

Cash in circulation

It is estimated that up to 75% of the cash circulating in the UK is drawn from a cash point machine and that on average each cash machine is used 1,500 times a week

Counterfeit money

By the end of the Civil War as much as half of the paper money in circulation in America was counterfeit, though steps taken reduced counterfeiting dramatically over the following decade. In 1980 777,957 counterfeit 50 and 100 dollar bills were seized by the authorities. In 1990, the number was 1,240,840, some 36% of which (in dollar value) had been produced overseas.

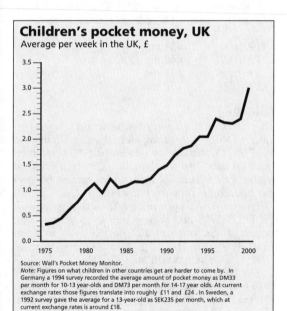

Children's pocket money, UK
Average per week in the UK, £

Source: Wall's Pocket Money Monitor.
Note: Figures on what children in other countries get are harder to come by. In Germany a 1994 survey recorded the average amount of pocket money as DM33 per month for 10-13 year-olds and DM73 per month for 14-17 year olds. At current exchange rates those figures translate into roughly £11 and £24 . In Sweden, a 1992 survey gave the average for a 13-year-old as SEK235 per month, which is around £18.

Credit card spending

According to Credit Card Research Group, credit card spending by the average Briton is the highest in Europe. In 1997 spending per head using credit cards was £1,675 in the UK, £1,360 in the Netherlands, £1,035 in France, £743 in Sweden, £473 in Ireland, £300 in Austria, £282 in Germany, Spain and Finland, £267 in Portugal, £260 in Belgium, £170 in Italy, £107 in Denmark and only £73 in Greece.

Forgotten or unclaimed money

The amount of money lying forgotten in dormant UK bank accounts could run into hundreds of millions of pounds according to estimates in June 2000. One bank alone, the Alliance and Leicester, disclosed that it had around £7m (nearly half a per cent of customer deposits).

In the United States an estimated $16 billion of forgotten funds are waiting to be claimed.

Unclaimed prizes in the UK national lottery amount to around 1% of sales and have been:

1995/96	£34 mn
1996/97	£48 mn
1997/98	£74 mn
1998/99	£78 mn

Gambling

The UK national lottery is the world's largest in value of sales, generating more than £5.5 billion in 1997/98. Of the money generated 50% was given out in prizes, 28% went to good causes, 13% went to the government in tax, retailers earned 5% and the operating company retained 4%.

The largest jackpot prize £42,008,610 was won on Jan 6 1996 and was shared by 3 tickets. The largest single prize of £22,590,829 was won on June 10 1996. The largest unclaimed prize of £2,054,754 was won on May 25 1996.

The biggest slot machine jackpot of $27,582,539 (£16,642,051) was won by a woman at the Palace Station Hotel and Casino, Las Vegas, Nevada, November 15 1998. She was a former flight attendant who had won $680,000 (£410,281) on another slot machine (The Wheel of Fortune Megajackpot) less than a month before.

Gold

The total amount of mined gold in the world is thought to be around 137,000 tonnes. If all the mined gold was formed into a cube it would fit under the first floor of the Eiffel Tower – the length of each side would be approximately that of a 22-yard cricket pitch.

As well as being scarce, gold is the most malleable and ductile of all metals. One tonne of gold could be formed into a thread that would stretch to the moon and back. One ounce could be beaten flat thin to cover one third of the Wembley Stadium soccer pitch.

Money laundering

The IMF estimate that money laundering may amount to between 2% and 5% of world GDP. On 1996 statistics this would translate into $590 billion and $1.5 trillion.

Wall Street Crash

In the four years from 1924, the Dow Jones index increase fourfold. In 1929 the market stalled; share prices slipped and then, as panic took over, went into freefall. The Dow lost 89% of its value and it took 26 years for US share prices to get back to their 1929 peak level.